THE TWO MOORS WAY

DEVON'S COAST TO COAST

About the Author

As soon as she could after leaving university, Sue grabbed the chance to return to Devon, where she spent 20 years commissioning walking, equestrian and countryside books for David & Charles Publishers. She started writing her first walking book three weeks after going freelance in 2000 and since then has written or contributed to around 20 books (and edited dozens more), specialising in her home territory of southwest England, especially Dartmoor and Exmoor. She writes the walks for *Exmoor: the country magazine*, and since 2008 has been editor (and is now co-owner) of *Dartmoor Magazine*.

Further afield she has walked across Corsica; in Madeira, the Canaries and the Balearics; scrambled in Snowdonia and Torridon; scaled the heights of Skye's Cuillin and Morocco's Atlas Mountains. She has also trekked to Everest Base Camp and in the Kanchenjunga region of Nepal, and most recently explored the fascinating high-plateau landscapes of Upper Mustang. Her first love, however, will always be the rolling green hills and atmospheric moorland of Devon, where she has lived for 35 years.

THE TWO MOORS WAY

DEVON'S COAST TO COAST

by Sue Viccars

2 POLICE SQUARE, MILNTHORPE, CUMBRIA LA7 7PY
www.cicerone.co.uk

© Sue Viccars 2015
First edition 2015
ISBN: 978 1 85284 714 2
Reprinted in 2017 (with updates)

Printed by KHL Printing, Singapore
A catalogue record for this book is available from the British Library.
Author photo © Stuart Wight.
All other photographs are by the author.

Dedication

For my boys, who love Devon too

Acknowledgements

Thanks as ever to all who have helped and kept me company on my various
ramblings (both on foot and verbal): to Brenda, Emma, Jackie and Stuart. Many
thanks too to all at Cicerone Press for their patience and hard work in producing
this guidebook.

Updates to this Guide

While every effort is made by our authors to ensure the accuracy of guidebooks
as they go to print, changes can occur during the lifetime of an edition. If we
know of any, they will be listed under the Updates tab on this book's page on
the Cicerone website (www.cicerone.co.uk/714/updates), so please check before
planning your trip. We also advise that you check information about such things
as transport, accommodation and shops locally. Even rights of way can be altered
over time. We are always grateful for information about any discrepancies between
a guidebook and the facts on the ground, sent by email to updates@cicerone.co.uk
or by post to Cicerone, 2 Police Square, Milnthorpe LA7 7PY, United Kingdom.

Front cover: Hamel Down from near Bel Tor Corner (Stage 4)

CONTENTS

Route symbols on OS map extracts
(for OS legend see printed OS maps)

 route

alternative route

 start point

 finish point

 alternative start point

alternative finish point

◀ route direction

Features on the overview map

———— County/Unitary boundary

Urban area

National Park

Area of Outstanding Natural Beauty

	400m
	200m
	75m
	0m

A South West Coast Path signpost marks the start of the route at Wembury beach (Stage 1)

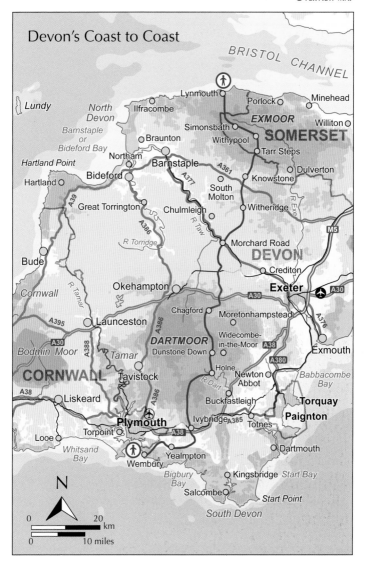

Looking back to Dartmoor from near Morchard Bishop, roughly halfway through the Two Moors Way (Stage 7)

INTRODUCTION

The Venton stone overlooks the Dane's Brook valley near Hawkridge, Exmoor (Stage 9)

Any long-distance walk from point-to-point brings with it a special sense of achievement, and a coast-to-coast is even better. Just look at the popularity of such routes as Wainwright's Coast to Coast, devised in the 1970s, from St Bee's Head in Cumbria to Robin Hood's Bay in North Yorkshire, or – more recently – the Hadrian's Wall Path National Trail, from Bowness-on-Solway to Wallsend on the Tyne.

But what about an option further south? A quick glance at the map reveals that England's southwest peninsula is the obvious place to look for a substantial coast-to-coast route, and that the best candidate for such an expedition is Devon. Not only is this England's third-largest county – allowing for a walk of over 100 miles (160km) – it is also the only one where the south and north coasts are separate and markedly different in character. And, being an essentially rural county and home to two of southwest England's unspoiled, magnificent and greatly contrasting moorlands – the granite heights of Dartmoor in the south, and softer Exmoor in the north – Devon can offer a route that takes walkers far off the beaten track for complete

The Two Moors Way stone at Stowford Bridge, Ivybridge (Stage 3)

immersion in this most delightful of counties.

Although Devon is undoubtedly a popular tourist destination the vast majority of visitors head for the coastal areas, and Mid Devon is quiet all year round. At Easter time and in the summer holidays 'honeypots' such as New Bridge on Dartmoor and Tarr Steps on Exmoor are thronged with visitors, but these are quickly passed to return to blissful solitude.

HISTORY OF THE ROUTE

The route known as 'Devon's Coast to Coast' is a combination of the well-known Two Moors Way and a section of the more recently established Erme–Plym Trail in South Devon. The creation of the former – a largely off-road walking route linking the two moors, running right across Dartmoor National Park and clipping the western edge of Exmoor – was the inspiration of Joe Turner, original chairman of the Two Moors Way Association. The appeal of Dartmoor and Exmoor for walkers has long been known. Although quite different in character, they both combine open common for a tougher challenge with a good network of lower-level valley rights of way for those wanting a less taxing day out.

The Two Moors Way was officially opened on 29 May 1976. Following Joe's death in 2004, Devon County

Council erected two memorial stones on the route as testament to his work. Dartmoor sculptor Peter Randall-Page's work is known throughout the world, and it is fitting that Joe's commitment should be commemorated in the form of a large worked granite 'boulder', divided in two. One half sits at the edge of the Exmoor section at Badlake Moor Cross alongside an engraved plaque celebrating the vision of Joe '...who created the route for all to enjoy'; its twin is positioned near the sculptor's home outside Drewsteignton, marking the Dartmoor section. These two sculptures face each other across the 30 miles (48km) of remote and rolling countryside that links Devon's two great moors.

In 2005 the Two Moors Way was officially linked with a section of the Erme–Plym Trail to form Devon's Coast to Coast route, running on to Wembury on the south coast. And although the complete route has now been up and running for ten years, people still tend to talk about it as 'the Two Moors Way – with that extra bit to the sea tacked on'! Hence the title and subtitle of this guidebook – but it is worth noting that the route does not stay entirely within the county bounds. The boundary between Devon and Somerset is crossed at Slade Bridge over the Dane's Brook south of Hawkridge (Stage 9), and Devon not regained until Stage 11.

Peter Randall-Page's sculpture at Badlake Moor Cross on Exmoor's southern edge (Stage 9)

GEOLOGY AND LANDSCAPE

Linking the Two Moors Way with the Erme–Plym Trail neatly adds another distinct landscape area to the original route, passing (from south to north) through the South Hams, Dartmoor, Mid Devon and Exmoor.

The South Hams

Starting from beautiful Wembury Bay on Devon's south coast, the first two stages of the route follow footpaths and bridleways through the rolling fields and copses of that part of South Devon known as the South Hams. The name is said to come from the Old English word *hām*, for an enclosed or sheltered space, which is perfectly appropriate: this is a gentle and unchallenging landscape. Geologically speaking, this area – stretching from Torbay in the east to Plymouth in the west – is comprised of Devonian slates, sandstones and limestones. Dating from 395 to 345 million years ago, the resulting green and gentle landscape stands in marked contrast to Dartmoor's brooding granite mass, encountered on Stage 3.

Dartmoor

Dartmoor (part of the same granite sheet that outcrops at Bodmin Moor and the West Penwith Moors in Cornwall, and further west in the Isles of Scilly) is essentially a raised plateau, and home to the highest wholly English mountain south of the Peak District. The plateau is tipped up and

drops south from its highest point – 2038ft (621m) at High Willhays – in the northwest corner.

Often evocatively described as 'the last wilderness in England' (although in truth the landscape represents thousands of years of interaction between man and nature), the moor can be a bleak and forbidding place, peppered with bizarrely sculpted granite tors, frequently shrouded in mist or battered by southwesterly gales, and hammered by an annual rainfall of over 90in (2286mm) on the western edge. The combination of high rainfall and thin acidic soil have over the centuries led to the creation of large areas of peat, resulting in extensive blanket bog on upland areas with slow run-off, now subject to a selective restoration project.

Dartmoor has the greatest concentration of Bronze Age sites in the country: the moor is studded with evidence of Bronze Age occupation in the form of hut circles (remnants of 'roundhouse' dwellings), single standing stones, and ceremonial structures such as stone circles or stone rows, the latter varying in length and consisting of a line of upright stones, many associated with burial kists (chambers). From medieval times tin was worked extensively, and the resulting pits and gullies are still visible today. Myths and legends abound: the witch Vixana, the famous 'Hairy Hands' and the Devil and his terrifying wisht hounds still blamed for all manner of strange happenings.

Bronze Age hut circle near Bel Tor Corner (Stage 4)

But around the edges of the plateau Dartmoor displays its softer side: sheltered wooded valleys created by sparkling rivers that have cut deeply into the less resistant shales and slates as they tumble off the unyielding granite; beautiful broadleaved woodland; a patchwork of small stone-walled fields and attractive hamlets.

Dartmoor National Park comprises an area of 368 square miles (953km²); the route described here enters the Park at Ivybridge, and leaves it just south of the A30. The High Moor (and extensive patches of blanket bog) are avoided, but the path still rises to 1736ft (532m) at Broad Burrow on Hamel Down (Stage 5). And walkers should note that Dartmoor always has

a trick up its sleeve... Whatever the weather, Ivybridge to Holne (Stage 3) is something of a challenge in terms of landscape, distance and – if visibility is poor – navigation!

Mid Devon

The land that lies between the two great moors – Mid Devon – is rarely visited. Hilly country criss-crossed by a complex network of narrow hedged lanes, scattered farms and hamlets, remote churches, a patchwork of small fields and pockets of woodland, this is 'real' rural Devon, far off the beaten track and untouched by the effects of tourism. Underlying Carboniferous rocks, laid down between 354 and 290 million years ago, support both fertile

13

farmland – where sandstone predominates, resulting in the characteristic red soils seen on Stages 6 and 7 in particular – and damp heathy grassland where the rocks are rich in shale.

Henry Williamson – author of the classic novel *Tarka the Otter* who lived in North Devon while recuperating after World War I – describes the countryside a little to the west of the route as 'the country covered by webbed paw, fin, clawed pad and pinion'. He captures the feel of this landscape perfectly.

Exmoor

Compared with Dartmoor's harsh granite, Exmoor's moorland plateau presents an altogether softer option.

Folded sedimentary rocks – sandstones and shales, among others – have produced smooth and rounded slopes, dissected by picturesque rivers running through steep-sided combes (similar to the Welsh *cwm*, meaning 'valley'). The story is altogether different at the coast: Exmoor's towering sea cliffs are the highest in England, making for a dramatic end to the walk at Lynmouth. And as on Dartmoor, Exmoor's highest ground can be a bleak and forbidding place in bad weather.

Although there is evidence of prehistoric activity it is less extensive and less obvious here than on Dartmoor, contributing to the sense of Exmoor being a more 'civilised' and ordered place. A greater proportion of the land

The River Barle north of Withypool (Stage 10)

The magnificent Foreland east of Lynmouth (Stage 11)

within the national park boundary is given over to farming, resulting in an essentially agricultural landscape of small walled fields, historic farmsteads and hamlets. Most Exmoor villages date from Saxon times.

The Two Moors Way crosses the Devonshire end of the national park, which covers 267 square miles (692km²) and extends east to include both the Brendon and Quantock Hills. It passes through part of the former Royal Forest, home to Exmoor ponies and red deer. Many of the characteristic manmade features of the Exmoor landscape – including miles of beautiful beech hedgebank (see 'Wildlife') – were created by the Knight family, who bought the King's Allotment,

the largest part of the Royal Forest, in 1818. The route runs alongside the lovely River Barle before crossing the watershed – the Chains, rising to 1599ft (487m) at Chains Barrow – near the source of Devon's great River Exe and passing through the boundary bank of the former Royal Forest. The last section of the walk climbs high above the dramatic wooded valley of the East Lyn before dropping steeply to the finish at Lynmouth, best-known for the terrible floods of 1952 when 34 people lost their lives.

The Royal Forests of Dartmoor and Exmoor

The route passes through a part of Exmoor that was designated 'Royal

Forest' in the 1200s and thereby set aside as a hunting ground for the king. The land was subject to Forest Law, and no buildings were allowed within the boundary.

Exmoor's Forest Court was held at Landacre (pronounced 'lannaker') Bridge near Withypool (Stage 10) and the duty of walking the boundary every seven years became an obligation of the 'free suitors, owners or tenants of the 52 tenements in the parishes of Hawkridge and Withypool'. In places it is still possible to trace the 31-mile (50km) boundary of the Royal Forest over open ground, particularly where it crosses the Chains, where stretches of a high bank, constructed along the line of the original boundary, are still visible. On Exmoor prehistoric barrows, stones, banks and trees were all used to denote the line of the boundary. The Hoar Oak tree (Stage 11) is the best-known and most obvious marker today.

Dartmoor's Royal Forest also dates from that time and was granted to the Black Prince – also the Duke of Cornwall – by Edward III in 1337, and the land has remained part of the Duchy of Cornwall ever since. The Forest lies within the parish of Lydford, which was the administrative centre. The boundary extends for roughly 52 miles (84km) and is marked by substantial stones, many of which can still be located. The earliest perambulation was recorded in 1240, and today makes for an excellent three-day walk across rough and pathless ground in the very heart of the moor. The route described in this guidebook touches the eastern edge of the Forest near Bennett's Cross (Stage 5).

WILDLIFE

Plants and flowers

All along the way – apart from on the open moorland stretches – readers will come across references to 'hedgebanks'. A Devon hedge (or hedgebank) is, just as it sounds, an earth bank, faced with stone or turf, topped with bushy vegetation. Many of Devon's hedges – the county has more than any other in the UK – date back over 800 years and support an astonishing range of plants, flowers and wildlife.

The moors support dancing white fluffy cotton grass in the summer months, sphagnum mosses and bright golden-yellow bog asphodel. Shady and undisturbed woodlands are thick with primroses, then bluebells, then wild garlic (ramsons) in spring and early summer, when Mid Devon's hedgerows put on a fine display of wildflowers and the prolific white blossoms of stunted hawthorns are

(opposite page, clockwise from top-left):
Lichen on hawthorn, Rowan (mountain ash) berries, Lichen on blackthorn,
Foxgloves, Common spotted orchid, Primroses, Dog violet, Broom, Bluebells

on show on the moors. Moving into autumn, the moors shimmer under a carpet of springy heather – common heather (ling), bell heather and cross-leaved heath – interspersed in places with stands of mustard-yellow Western gorse. Mountain ash sports heavy clumps of bright-red-orange berries; and Exmoor's beech hedgebanks glow orange and brown as shorter hours of daylight (and thus a reduction in chlorophyll) lead to a predominance of red and yellow compounds in the leaves.

One species that grows in profusion on both moors is the humble whortleberry (bilberry or blaeberry, known locally as 'whort'), its blue-grey berries ready for picking in August. A hundred years or so ago, picking whorts was an important seasonal industry, and during World War I the berries were used to dye military uniforms. Schoolchildren were given time off to help with the harvest, and the berries were sold at local markets and to dealers travelling from as far away as London.

Birds and animals

On the moorland stretches walkers are accompanied by the rich song of the skylark in spring and summer; throughout the route look out for buzzards gliding high in the sky. Blanket bog restoration projects on both moors are intended to encourage the breeding of wading birds such as curlew and dunlin: Dartmoor holds the last remaining population of breeding dunlin in southern England.

Think Dartmoor, and you think of Dartmoor ponies. A pony was chosen as the logo of the national park in 1951, and Dartmoor's hill ponies are still one of the moor's biggest attractions for visitors; walkers on the Two Moors Way are likely to find them on Hamel Down and around Bennett's Cross (Stage 5). The pony situation is complicated in that historically what might be thought of as a 'true' Dartmoor pony has been interbred with other breeds to produce the mix, including black/brown and white animals, seen on the commons today. Some may be Heritage ponies, nearer to the true breed, which is characteristically bay or brown, with little or no white marking. The Dartmoor Pony Society was set up in 1925 to protect the registered Dartmoor Pony.

All Dartmoor's hill ponies are owned by someone with common grazing rights, and are rounded up each October for the annual drift sale at Chagford, at which some are sold, and some youngstock microchipped and returned to the moor. But keeping ponies is no longer financially viable for most people and numbers have dropped from around 30,000 in the 1950s to fewer than 1500 animals today. Organisations such as The Dartmoor Hill Pony Association (www.dartmoorhillpony.com) and the Dartmoor Pony Heritage Trust (www.dpht.co.uk) are working to secure the future of ponies on the moor.

On Exmoor the situation is rather different. Over the generations

Dartmoor hill pony mare and foal

steps have been taken to maintain the original breed standard, and so those animals seen today are 'true' Exmoors, officially recognised as an endangered species of native pony, are typified by their stocky build, brown colour, dark mane and tail, mealy muzzle and eye patch. Some of the hardy Exmoors seen on the moor today are descendants of the Anchor herd of 30 animals taken from the Royal Forest to Winsford Hill, above Tarr Steps, by warden Sir Thomas Dyke Acland in 1818 when part of the Forest was sold to John Knight. By 1946 only 50 ponies remained, but today there are estimated to be around 3000 worldwide. The Moorland Mousie Trust runs the Exmoor Pony Centre near Dulverton

(www.moorlandmousietrust.org. uk). Walkers are particularly likely to come across Exmoor ponies in the Landacre Bridge area above the River Barle on Stage 10.

Although stock levels on both Dartmoor and Exmoor have been significantly reduced over the last few years, there are also cattle and sheep on some of the moorland stages. On Dartmoor you will come across South Devon, Belted Galloway, Galloway and Highland cattle, as well as Scotch Blackface and Whiteface Dartmoor sheep, while characteristic native breeds of sheep likely to be seen on the Exmoor stages include Scotch Blackface and Exmoor, alongside Ruby Red Devon and Welsh Black cattle.

19

Exmoor pony mare

Highland cattle on Shapley Common (Stage 5)

Exmoor is home to the greatest number of red deer in England. A stag's head is used as the national park's logo, and many pubs and hotels are adorned with hunting trophies in the form of mounted antlers and hooves. Britain's largest land animal, red deer are thought to be have been present in the area since prehistoric times, and number around 3000 today.

And finally mention should be made of the otter, which, following a steady decline during the 1950s and 1960s, has now been recorded on every river in Devon. You would be fantastically lucky to spot one, but you may find evidence of their presence in the form of footprints or spraint (dung) on riverbanks or riverside rocks, used by the otter to mark its territory.

WHEN TO GO

There are two major considerations when thinking about the best time of year to tackle the route: season and weather.

Season

Devon is one of the UK's most popular tourist destinations, and population figures soar during the holiday season. The 2011 census recorded a total of over a million residents in a county which gets up to five million visitors a year. Annual visitor figures do vary – largely depending on how good the weather was the previous summer – but during the peak season there is a huge increase in local

traffic and demand on local facilities. The vast majority of visitors, however, head for the coastal resorts, and walkers on the route will, for the most part, be blissfully unaware of the tourist season. Dartmoor has around 2.4 million visitors a year, and Exmoor 1.4 million, but very few are likely to be found crossing the moors on foot.

Do be aware, however, that accommodation at the start and finish, and on the Dartmoor and Exmoor stretches, is harder to find at Easter and during the summer holidays. And in any case, accommodation along the way is limited; never rely on turning up unannounced at a B&B or pub and being guaranteed a place to stay for the night. Some accommodation providers close during the 'off' season (between the end of October half-term break and Easter) but may reopen over Christmas and New Year, often charging a premium.

Weather

England's southwest peninsula is blessed with a relatively balmy climate due to the moderating influence of the surrounding sea, and Devon and Cornwall experience the highest average year-round temperatures in Britain. Temperature varies with location, and the South Hams sections of the route (Stages 1 and 2) would typically enjoy higher temperatures than those across Dartmoor and Exmoor; average temperatures for Exmoor, for example, are stated as ranging from about 15°C (59°F) in August to about

The upper Chains valley (Stage 11)

5°C (41°F) in February. But these are only averages, and summer temperatures on both moors are often pleasantly warm, usually tempered by a light breeze.

The statistic that is of most concern to walkers is average rainfall. Devon's location puts it at the mercy of regular Atlantic depressions, driven by the prevailing southwesterly winds, which batter the coasts and moors, especially during the winter months. Rainfall totals have a surprisingly large range, depending on the lie of the land: the annual rainfall at Princetown, 1475ft (450m) above sea level on Dartmoor, is around double Plymouth's figure of around 44in (940mm), and in 2013 Holne received

a whacking 84.9in (2155.5mm)! Even across a relatively small area rainfall varies greatly. On Dartmoor in 2013 February was the driest month on the South Moor, whereas it was July on the North Moor. Exmoor is similarly unpredictable, with the Chains (crossed on Stage 11) receiving around 80in (2030mm) per annum, and the driest months tending to be May and June.

But the climate is notoriously fickle and even in the height of summer low cloud and a steady drizzle can ruin a day on Dartmoor or Exmoor, destroying any chance of a view and making navigation tricky. Although on both moors people still talk about the terrible snows of the winter of 1962–63, when moorland farms were cut off for months, in recent years very low winter temperatures and snowfall, even on the very highest ground (other than over a couple of weeks in the winter of 2011–12), have been a rarity. The Met Office website (www.metoffice.gov.uk) gives the most accurate weather forecasts for the region.

In general, late spring and early summer (April to the end of June) and autumn (September and October) are the best months to go (outside the peak holiday times). From April to early June the woodlands of the South Hams and Mid Devon are awash with primroses, bluebells and ramsons in quick succession; the moors are dotted with pony foals, lambs and calves and blessed with the evocative song of the skylark; the pinky-green leaves of the oak woodlands of the East Lyn valley almost glow in the spring sunshine. From late August onwards walkers can admire a carpet of rich purple heather on the moorland stretches and the amazing oranges and browns of beech and oak in the wooded valleys; the leaves tend to stay on the trees until well into November.

PLANNING THE WALK

Having decided when to go, you need to think how you are going to organise your trip. Are you planning

Oak tree and buttercups on the track to Pyne Farm (Stage 7)

Washfood Woods in late May (Stage 7)

an unsupported yomp across the county, bivvying at night and pushing on as far as physically possible each day, taking potluck on finding somewhere to camp? Do you have limited time available and want to cover the route in five or six days? Would you prefer to take things more gently and stay at a comfortable B&B or pub, but have your overnight luggage transported to your next port of call? Can you persuade a friend to drop you off at the start of each day's walk, and pick you up at the end? Or perhaps you would rather book your trip through a company that can organise the whole trip for you (see Appendix D)?

South to north – or north to south?

The route directions in this guide have been written from south to north, starting at Wembury and finishing at Lynmouth. Each direction has its share of devotees with sound reasons for their preference. It is true that the distant views of Dartmoor's granite bulk are more impressive than those of Exmoor's sandstone slopes, which lends weight to the north–south option. But anyone tackling the route from the Lynmouth end is immediately faced with a long and steep climb from the coast to the top of the East Lyn ravine – around 800ft (250m) – enough to deter even the most enthusiastic walker!

Before the Two Moors Way was linked to the Erme–Plym Trail there was a certain appeal in starting at Ivybridge and finishing at the sea. Now that the additional 16½ miles (26.6km) from Wembury have been added, walking from south to north gives a pleasant one or two days of easy walking before tackling the long and sometimes challenging stage across Dartmoor from Ivybridge to Holne. If the weather is behaving, the prevailing southwesterlies should help to push south–north walkers on their way, rather than beat them in the face. There is also the advantage that public transport access to Wembury and the start of the route is better, and transport links to nearby Plymouth good. And the last section of the final stage brings with it some of the most spectacular scenery experienced on the entire journey, and a wonderful sense of anticipation as Lynmouth, tucked under Exmoor's extraordinary hog's-back cliffs, is approached at the end of the route.

How many miles?
Assessments of the precise mileage of both the Two Moors Way and the complete Devon Coast to Coast route seem to vary. The Devon County Council booklet claims 102 miles (164km) for the Two Moors Way (as does the signpost outside The Watermark in Ivybridge, the official start/finish point) and 117 miles (187km) for the whole route. Previously published guidebooks offer different figures.

Distances for this guidebook have been measured by GPS and the Erme–Plym section comes out at 16½ miles (26.6km) and Two Moors Way at 99¾ miles (160.5km), making the complete Devon Coast to Coast 116¼ miles (187km)!

ACCOMMODATION

Overnight accommodation must be booked in advance. Spend some time looking online and making phone calls. It may be that you can find accommodation a few miles away from the end of a stage; many B&B owners will agree to come and pick you up, and drop you off again the following morning (and provide you with a packed lunch).

Appendix C lists some selected accommodation options along the Way and Appendix D gives details of tourist information offices and village websites which list accommodation in the local area. Recently, the Two Moors Way Association has been revived, and a new website (www.twomoorsway.org) created: check it out for information on accommodation and on all aspects of organising the walk. Another website covering the whole route is www.ramblefest.com (although this is not completely up-to-date). Some of the companies that sell organised trips along the route also list accommodation options on their websites.

Another option is to book a few days in self-catering accommodation

Tarr Steps is one of Exmoor's most popular tourist attractions (Stages 9 and 10)

and stay there while tackling three or four stages. Most such providers will be prepared to consider a short let out of season. You will need a party with two cars or a willing assistant to drop you off at the start and pick you up at the end of the day; rural southwest England is not blessed with a comprehensive and regular public transport network.

Walking from point to point and staying overnight will involve transporting your own luggage, but many accommodation providers will offer to move your luggage on for you, for a fee. Check at the time of booking. It is also possible to pre-book your luggage transfer with a company such as the appropriately named Luggage

Transfers based in Helston, Cornwall (www.luggagetransfers.co.uk), but this adds considerably to the cost of your trip. You can also arrange pick up and drop off for yourself as well.

If in the end you find sorting out the trip yourself too daunting you can try one of the companies offering self-guided trips, which will arrange accommodation and luggage transfer according to your specific itinerary. Encounter Holidays (www.encounterwalkingholidays.com) based in Lerryn in Cornwall run a variety of different options, depending on how far you want to walk each day, and their website has a lot of useful information on the route. See Appendix D for details of other companies.

Wild camping on Dartmoor

Dartmoor is the only national park in England where wild camping is allowed, but there are still rules. A downloadable map is available via the national park website, which details where you can and cannot camp, or where camping is allowed but you still need to get the landowner's permission. Lightweight tents only are allowed, and should not be pitched within 100m of a road, be visible from the roadside or any property, on farmland or moorland enclosed within walls, on flood plains or archaeological sites. See www.dartmoor-npa. gov.uk for more information. Wild camping is not allowed anywhere on Exmoor and anyone wishing to camp should get the landowner's permission in advance. The term 'common land' does not automatically imply a right to camp.

PUBLIC TRANSPORT

In general terms public transport across the more rural parts of Devon (and that part of Somerset encountered on this route) is poor. Bus services to remote villages are at best infrequent and irregular, at worst non-existent. The route has a brief flirtation with the national rail network at Ivybridge and Morchard Road, but as an almost totally rural route across what is relatively remote countryside it does not enjoy the benefits of good

The path runs along Dartmoor's Hamel Down ridge (Stage 5)

public transport links. Those walkers tackling the route in a piecemeal way and who need to use public transport to reach the start and leave the finish of each stage will find details of what is available (if anything) at the start of each stage description. Details of how to access the start and finish of the entire route using public transport are given under 'Getting there and getting away'. The overall message has to be this: other than for reaching the start and leaving the finish of the route do not rely on public transport as an integral part of the planning process.

MAPS

The OS Explorer 1:25,000 series is recommended for this walk, and the relevant maps are:
• OL20 South Devon
• OL28 Dartmoor
• 113 Okehampton
• 127 South Molton & Chulmleigh
• 114 Exeter & the Exe Valley
• OL9 Exmoor

Note that only a tiny section of the route (within Stage 7) appears on Explorer 127. The relevant Landranger 1:50,000 maps for the region (which are adequate, although less detailed than the Explorer series) are:
• 201 Plymouth & Launceston
• 202 Torbay & South Dartmoor
• 191 Okehampton & North Dartmoor
• 181 Minehead & Brendon Hills
• 180 Barnstaple & Ilfracombe

Harvey Maps also produce a 1:40,000 map of Dartmoor, and one specifically on the Two Moors Way, covering Stages 3–11.

GETTING THERE AND GETTING AWAY

It's important to think about how to make this route work for you, and how best to access both start and finish. If tackling the route independently, you must work it all out in advance. Arriving in Lynmouth at the end of the long walk from Simonsbath on a drizzly evening only to find you've missed the last bus 'out' would be an unfortunate end to a wonderful walk. It may be that you have a willing friend who is prepared to drop you off in Wembury early one morning and pick you up in Lynmouth however many days later, but if that isn't the case there are various options available. All local travel options are available on www.travelinesw.com, but the following information should also help with planning.

The start

Wembury can be accessed in a number of different ways from Plymouth, which is on the main Paddington–Penzance railway line, operated by First Great Western (www.firstgreatwestern.co.uk). It's about a 10-minute walk from the station to Royal Parade in the city centre, from which the local bus to Wembury can be caught; most of the buses

Looking up the Avon valley from the descent to the clapper bridge at Huntingdon Warren (Stage 3)

passing the station will take you to Royal Parade too. Alternatively, you could get off the train at Ivybridge and take a taxi to Wembury. Plymouth and Ivybridge are served by National Express coaches (www. nationalexpress.com), a cheaper option than travelling by train.

- **By car** Wembury is signed off the A379 in the centre of Elburton, 4 miles (6.4km) east of Plymouth city centre, or 4½ miles (7.2km) from Marsh Mills roundabout on the A38. There is no long-term parking in the National Trust car park at Wembury Beach.

- **By taxi** Taxi First in Plymouth (01752 222222 www.taxifirst.net) transports walkers from the station to Wembury for around £11.50; the return trip to Plymouth (or a drop-off at Taunton for the mainline railway) at the end of the walk costs £111. Try also Wembury Cars (01752 881651), around £12, which also offers B&B accommodation (one twin room); Ivy Cabs (01752 696969 www.ivycabs.co.uk) in Ivybridge (around £25 from Ivybridge station to Wembury); or South Hams Travel (0800 1934000), which does the Plymouth–Wembury run for around £20 (all prices 2014).

The beach at Wembury: the start of the cross-county route can be accessed from Plymouth via the South West Coast Path (Stage 1)

- **By bus** First bus no 48 from Plymouth city centre via Plymstock; the nearest stop to the start of the route is on Church Road, ½ mile from the coast at the bottom of Wembury village.

- **On foot** If you can add an extra day (and are happy to spend a night in Wembury) to your trip you can walk to the start of the route from Plymouth via the South West Coast Path.

The Coast Path option

If you want to broaden your Devon walking experience, tack on a day or two at the start and enjoy walking a stretch of the South West Coast Path. Catch a bus from the city centre to Plymouth's historic Barbican and take the Mount Batten Ferry, which runs from near Mayflower Steps to Mount Batten Pier on the east side of Cattewater at the mouth of the River Plym. The ferries leave the Barbican at a quarter to and a quarter past the hour, all year round (weather permitting); check the timetable at www. mountbattenferry.com. Make sure you have small change for the fare (£1.50 in 2014). (First bus no 2 also runs to Mount Batten Pier from the city centre.) From the ferry pontoon turn right to pick up Coast Path signs and walk the 7¼ miles (11.6km) to Wembury.

The settlements passed on the route may not be the most picturesque, but the way is packed with historic sites that emphasise the strategic importance of Plymouth and its huge natural harbour, from the mid-17th-century Mount Batten tower, built in response to a threat of war with the Dutch, to Bovisand Fort, constructed in the mid-19th century to defend the entrance to Plymouth Sound. The coastal scenery becomes increasingly dramatic around Bovisand and beyond to Wembury Point, before a run of low cliffs edges Wembury Bay, heavily battered during the winter storms of early 2014. There is a good selection of cafés and pubs at regular intervals along the route, including the bright and cheerful Cliffedge Café at Bovisand, which is open all year round. Stay overnight in Wembury, then set off on the Coast to Coast route the following day.

The finish

Getting home from Lynmouth at the end of the walk should also be worked out in advance. Once again this part of North Devon is not blessed with an extensive public transport network (although services do increase slightly during the summer high season), so make sure you have planned your 'escape'.

- **By car** Lynmouth is a popular tourist spot sited on the A39 and as such has plenty of facilities for visitors. If you have arranged to be picked up at the end of the walk, there are plenty of public car parks in which to meet your private 'taxi'; if you want to leave a car in Lynmouth before getting to Wembury to start the walk, one-week or four-day parking tickets are available from the tourist information centre (£20/£13, 2015 prices). Between 1 November and Good Friday there is also free on-street parking available in Lynton. Note that the easiest (but costliest) way of getting to Wembury to start the route is by taxi – but that there are lengthy bus and train/coach options: see below.

- **By taxi** Lyn Valley Taxi (01598 753800 or 07907 161666 email: lynvalleytaxi@aol.com www. lynvalleytaxi.co.uk) on Park Street, Lynton, undertakes both local and long-distance hops and has an eight-seater vehicle available for bigger parties. They transport walkers to Taunton for main rail and bus links, and even make the journey down to Wembury to collect walkers. Coastline Taxis (01598 753424 or 07891 876408 email: coastlinetaxislynton@hotmail.co.uk www.coastlinetaxis. wordpress.com: phone for a quote), also in Lynton, offer a similar service. Escape the City Tours, based in Ilfracombe, offer an eight-seater taxi service to and from Taunton and Tiverton railway stations (01271 410080 email: enquiries@escapethecitytours. co.uk www.escapethecitytours. co.uk).

- **By bus** Current bus timetables can be downloaded from the tourist information centre website www. lynton-lynmouth-tourism.co.uk and the County Council website has full information and an interactive bus map (www.devon.gov. uk/buses.htm). Local bus services tend to come up for tender each year, but although the provider may change the service numbers tend to stay the same. The 310 and 309 services run to Barnstaple,

Monday to Saturday (to link with the Tarka Line railway to Exeter); the 300 (daily) goes to Minehead, then service 28 can be ridden to Taunton for mainline railway and bus services. These services run roughly three times a day.

- **On foot** From Lynmouth the South West Coast Path stretches along the coastal hills of Devon and Somerset west for 15 miles (24.1km) to Combe Martin and east for 12½ miles (20.1km) to Porlock Weir: great options for anyone wishing to extend their walking trip with one more wonderful day along the coast. Make sure, however, that once again

The River Erme flows through the Flete estate (Stage 2)

you plan your escape from your final destination in advance.

WHAT TO TAKE

Whatever the time of year, and however settled and dry the weather may seem, do not trust it. England's southwest peninsula is at the mercy of the Atlantic depressions, and it often rains. Carry good waterproofs (jacket and trousers) all year round, as well as gloves and a hat: you need to be prepared should the weather turn as you're about to embark on Stage 3, even in midsummer. Gaiters are recommended for the moorland sections other than in the very driest of conditions. Walking poles are useful for negotiating rough ground and moorland stream crossings, especially after heavy rainfall.

Boots or tough walking shoes – although not essential for the Erme–Plym stages – are highly recommended for the moorland sections and also for Mid Devon in anything other than very dry weather since many paths and field gateways are pretty much permanently wet and muddy.

Other than the above the usual items such as food and drink, an extra warm layer, map, compass, guidebook, GPS, camera, first-aid kit, notebook and mobile phone should be carried. In hot, sunny weather wear a sunhat and apply sunscreen to exposed areas.

FOOD AND DRINK

Rural Devon is not, as many might like to think, furnished with a cosy village shop and pub in every picturesque village or hamlet. Scores of village shops and post offices have closed, and despite a relatively recent upsurge in the number of community shops, largely run by volunteers – such as the one in Holne (Stage 3), perfectly positioned right on the route, and with a tearoom – the majority of smaller villages passed do not have any such facilities. Take heed of the advice given at the start of each stage description about whether or not it is possible to pick up supplies during the day and, if in any doubt, ask your accommodation provider (in advance) to prepare a packed lunch for you.

Likewise carry enough water for the day, taking into account the temperature, and do not fill water bottles from streams.

HEALTH AND SAFETY

This is not a particularly challenging route in terms of terrain – any steep ascents or slippery descents tend to be relatively short and sweet – and the stages can, to a certain extent, be adjusted to suit varying levels of walking ability. There is, however, no way of shortening or adapting Stage 3, the long haul across the open moor from Ivybridge to Scorriton. This can be something of a slog, and most of the stage is across open moorland, and the latter part pathless. The advantage

Western gorse carpets the slopes of the Dart valley (Stage 4)

of such terrain is that you get a real feel for Dartmoor 'proper'; the disadvantage is that if the mist is down and conditions poor you will need to use map and compass to navigate your way safely on the stretch between the Red Lake track and leaving the moor at Chalk Ford. An alternative valley route (Stage 5A) is offered to enable walkers to avoid the Hamel Down ridge (Stage 5) in poor conditions, but the same problem arises on Stage 11 when the route crosses Exmoor's highest ground (The Chains), where map and compass will again be needed in poor visibility.

Other than that, walkers of average fitness should have no difficulties, barring an unfortunate and unpredictable sprained ankle or bashed knee. Heed the usual advice about protecting yourself from the sun on hot summer days, and carry sufficient water to avoid getting dehydrated (refilling your water bottle from a moorland stream is never recommended unless you are carrying water-purifying tablets or a neutralising device). Likewise, if tackling the route in the cooler months, be aware that wind chill on the moors can drop the temperature by several degrees: make sure you have adequate warm and waterproof clothing with you.

Remember that any ponies encountered on the commons of Dartmoor and Exmoor are wild and, however inquisitive they may appear, should not be approached or fed.

Avoid mares with very young foals and cattle with calves, especially if you have a dog. From springtime onwards adders may be seen basking on dry sections of path on warm sunny days, and should be left undisturbed.

And if you do bring a dog with you be aware that you need to keep it on a lead when crossing the moors or walking through fields of livestock during the lambing and bird-nesting season (1 March to 31 July), and under close control at all other times.

Coping with ticks

These nasty little blood-sucking parasites lurk in areas of bracken, long grass and low-growing whortleberry, all of which are prevalent on the moorland areas encountered on this route. Ticks are not only an unpleasant irritation but on rare occasions a victim may develop Lyme's disease, which can have unpleasant consequences (see www.lymediseaseaction.org.uk). Avoid picking up ticks by wearing long trousers tucked into socks (or gaiters), and take something with you to sit on when taking a break. Ticks should be removed with tweezers held firmly around the creature, close to the skin, and a steady, upward pulling motion employed. The affected area should be treated with disinfectant.

The path runs alongside the beautiful River Barle (Stage 10)

The walker will come across a great variety in design and quality of signage!

MOBILE PHONES AND EMERGENCIES

In the unfortunate event of a real emergency on the moors both Dartmoor and Exmoor field Search and Rescue teams, which assist the police on emergency call outs: see Appendix D for contact details. Dial 112 or 999 and ask for the police. You need to register your mobile phone before being able to alert the emergency services by text message: for more information visit www.emergencysms.org.uk (this service is provided for those with hearing difficulties or impaired speech).

Be aware too that you are not guaranteed mobile reception everywhere along the route, and particularly not on parts of the moorland stretches or in deep and wooded valleys.

WAYMARKING AND ACCESS

When the Erme–Plym extension was added to the Two Moors Way, the Wembury–Ivybridge section was comprehensively waymarked, and walkers should have no problems following the route.

On the moorland sections the signage situation is markedly different. There are no access issues; on Dartmoor the Two Moors Way was deliberately routed so as to avoid the military ranges in the west and northwest of the moor, which, although not closed to the public as such, should not be entered during times of military training activity. But whereas there are specific rights of way across both moors defined on the map, on the ground it's not quite so simple. Do not expect clear waymarking on either moor: there may be discrete signs where a bridleway leads across the common from a road, for example, but generally there is no helpful signage on the open moor. The route north from Ivybridge on Dartmoor initially follows a clear track, and the point at which the route turns off is marked by an engraved stone, but no further sign of any sort is picked up until the moor is left en route to Scorriton. Follow the directions carefully across these stretches of unsigned ground.

In Mid Devon the route follows designated rights of way. Some footpath and bridleway signs are adorned with a Two Moors Way symbol of varying ages and conditions. At other times you may follow a signed right of way with no indication that it is part of the Devon Coast to Coast route. The Mid Devon section is also fairly user-friendly, because where the route runs along field edges there is usually a decent-width strip left uncultivated to accommodate walkers. These grassy walkways are a joy because in summer, when some fields are filled with barley or maize, it is not necessary to struggle along a rough and narrow path, squeezed in between crops and the hedgebank and impeded by nettles and brambles.

The Mewstone sits just off the coast at Wembury (Stage 1)

USING THIS GUIDE

The Devon Coast to Coast does not break down into neat little stages of equal distance, and how you choose to organise the trip comes down to personal preference (and how overnight stops can be organised).

This guidebook splits the route into 11 stages, as shown in the route summary table in Appendix A. These 11 stages are, to a certain extent, dictated by the lie of the land. There is no way of shortening Stage 3, for example: 13½ miles (21.75km) across southern Dartmoor from Ivybridge to Holne. But if Stage 6 – 18 miles (29km) from Chagford Bridge to Morchard Road – feels like too much of a stretch there is the option of either pushing on for a few miles at the end of Stage 5 and staying in Drewsteignton, or of breaking Stage 6 around the 11-mile (17.7km) mark (the left turn to Newbury) and walking on for an extra mile or two to Yeoford. Those who want to complete the route more quickly can combine two shorter stages, for example get Wembury to Ivybridge over with in one long day (16½ miles/26.6km), or push on to Chagford at the end of Stage 4 (16¾ miles/27km), rather than overnighting somewhere in the Dunstone Down/Widecombe area. Appendix B provides a breakdown of each stage into shorter sections to give more flexibility in the planning process.

Each stage gives details of start and finish points (with grid references), plus distance in miles and kilometres and an estimate of time (including stops for refreshment and to take photographs). It must be emphasised that this figure is only a guide: individuals know how fast they walk and how many rest stops they are likely to take, and a larger party tends to have a slower rate of progress than a single walker or couple. On most of the stages inclement weather does not unduly affect the rate of progress, but on the more exposed moorland sections – Stages 3 and 11 – strong winds and rain do impede progress. Despite the prevailing southwesterlies, on rare occasions a strong northerly or northwesterly wind can be experienced while trudging up the old Red Lake Railway on Stage 3, which can add a surprising number of minutes to the estimated time.

An idea of the terrain to be traversed is given, and the recommended OS Explorer 1:25,000 and Landranger 1:50,000 map listed for each stage. The Explorer series is always the preferred option.

Refreshment options and toilets on the route are listed, and also those a short distance off the path. Where walkers need to stock up with food and drink for the day before setting out in the morning, a note is included at the start of the route directions. In some cases there is no chance to buy anything either in the morning or at the end of the pervious day's walk, and in such cases careful forward planning is required; many B&Bs and pubs will knock up a sandwich or two and provide a packet of crisps for a takeaway picnic if asked in advance.

Details of public transport to start and finish points are given, for those walkers not planning to walk the whole route in one go. Consult Traveline (see Appendix D) for more detailed information, and be aware that several stops along the route have no public transport worth listing: Widecombe, for example, is served by one bus a week, and that only goes to Newton Abbot to tie in with the livestock market every Wednesday. Finally an idea of where to park is given, once again for those doing the walk in daily stages and either leaving a car at the end of the stage, or needing to be picked up by a willing accomplice.

Alternative route options

On some stages, where appropriate, an alternative route is suggested for a short way. The OS Explorer map for Dartmoor, for example, marks two different options in the Widecombe area: the main route along the Hamel Down ridge from Dunstone Down and a second route up the East Webburn valley to the east. In this guide alternative routes are given only where there is good reason for doing so: the valley route mentioned above (Stage 5A) is described because it gives a sensible low-level option for when the cloud is low on Hamel Down. (Unfortunately, the one stage that really could benefit from a low-level moorland-edge alternative is Stage 3 across the southern moor, but there is no obvious way of creating one.)

High water after heavy rainfall, and therefore difficult or impossible stream or river crossings, is likely to be the biggest problem on the moorland sections. For that reason two short alternatives are offered to avoid crossing the Western Wella Brook at Huntingdon Warren when in spate (Stage 3), and an alternative high-level route suggested on Stage 9 (avoiding Tarr Steps and giving an alternative finish point in Withypool) and also on Stage 10, recommended if the Barle is running excessively high along its valley south of Simonsbath. Of these three the one most likely to cause a problem (and the simplest to get around) is the Western Wella Brook.

STAGE 1
Wembury to Yealmpton

Start	Wembury Beach (SX 517 485)
Finish	Yealmpton, crossroads on the A379 in village centre (SX 579 518)
Distance	7½ miles (12km)
Time	4hrs
Terrain	Rolling fields and wooded valleys
Maps	Explorer OL20 South Devon; Landranger 201 Plymouth & Launceston, 202 Torbay & South Dartmoor
Refreshments	The Old Mill Café, Wembury Beach; The Odd Wheel Inn, Wembury (off route); Mary Green General Store, Brixton Fish and Chips and The Foxhound pub, Brixton; Riverford Farm Shop and Café, Kitley (off route); Market Street Café, Village Stores, Rose & Crown pub and The Volunteer pub, Yealmpton
Public toilets	Wembury (opposite The Old Mill Café)
Public transport	For Wembury: Plymouth–Wembury bus service; for Yealmpton: Plymouth–Dartmouth and Plymouth–Newton Ferrers bus services
Parking	National Trust car park, Wembury Beach (members free); roadside in Yealmpton
Accommodation	B&B, camping

On a sunny day it's easy to linger a little longer than intended at the lovely beach at Wembury, starting point for Devon's Coast to Coast: it's a stunning stretch of coastline, and the foreshore is of international importance on account of its marine life. Give yourself enough time to visit the Marine Centre (free entry, seasonal opening); and pick up a pasty from the Old Mill Café to keep you going. But once you've set off on the Erme–Plym Trail all thoughts of coastal walking are soon left behind as a delightful run of sweeping fields and wooded valleys is encountered. Surprisingly early on in the route come far-reaching views towards the southern slopes of Dartmoor and the official start of the Two Moors Way at Ivybridge.

Minehead is signed 424 miles to the west, and Poole 206 miles to the east.

The Erme–Plym Trail is picked up where it leaves the South West Coast Path at the back of Wembury Beach. ◄

The **Great Mewstone** sits off Wembury Point and has an interesting story to l. In 1744 a convicted felon was 'deported' to the island, with his family, for seven years. When he left, his daughter 'Black Joan' decided to stay, only leaving the island when her husband fell off a rock and drowned. The artist JMW Turner immortalised the island in watercolour in around 1813; and the last inhabitant left in 1850. After World War II it was purchased by the War Office, and since 2006 has been owned by the National Trust as a bird colony.

map continues on page 46

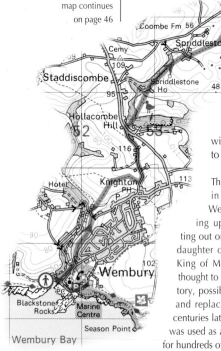

Tear yourself away from the sea and set off inland, almost immediately passing through a gate. The broad path leads upvalley through grasses and wildflowers, eventually bearing right to a small gate onto a lane.

The **church of St Werburgh** stands in a prominent position above Wembury Beach; it's worth climbing up there for a look before setting out on your walk. Werburgh was the daughter of Wulfhere, the first Christian King of Mercia. The present building is thought to stand on the site of a Saxon oratory, possibly dating from the 9th century and replaced by a Norman church three centuries later. The early 15th-century tower was used as a navigation landmark by sailors for hundreds of years.

Take time to visit St Werburgh's Church before setting off

Turn left to the lane junction and cross Church Road to continue up a concrete track, on a bridleway, to reach a house. Follow the path left, gently uphill, to a junction; keep ahead on the bridleway (often muddy). ▶ On meeting a deeply banked lane turn left, downhill.

At the time of writing an old footpath running parallel to it had fallen into disuse.

In the valley bottom cross a ford; just before the lane bears right turn right up a track past Ford Farm. At track end keep straight on along a narrow path that ascends to a footpath post and path junction. Keep straight on, uphill (tall foxgloves in summer) to cross a stile into a big field. Bear right along the edge to cross a V-stile by a gate, then keep right along the next field edge. ▶

At the top pass through a small gate into an arable field and bear half left across it (in summer a clear strip is left for walkers) to reach a path junction at an open gateway; keep ahead on a broad field track.

Look out for meadow brown butterflies and house martins in high summer.

The substantial 16th-century building seen away to the left from these fields is **Langdon Court Hotel** (one of four manors in the area originally recorded

South Devon cattle in rolling pasture below Hollacombe Wood

The Odd Wheel Inn is a few minutes' walk down the lane to the right.

in the Domesday Book). In the mid 16th century the house was given to Catherine Parr, widow of Henry VIII.

At the next hedge gap bear diagonally right across the field, passing just left of a telegraph pole, and descend to a V-stile onto the lane (Traine Road) at the top of Wembury village. ◀ Turn left, uphill. The lane levels off and soon meets the busier Wembury Road at **Hollacombe**.

Suddenly the **southern scarp of Dartmoor** – stretching for around over 40 miles (64km) from Lee Moor in the west, northeast to Haytor – appears in all its glory in the distance. The divide between Dartmoor's resistant granite and the softer Devonian slates and shales of the South Hams is clear to see. Butterdon Hill, rising to 1204ft (367m) above Ivybridge, marks the first section of the Two Moors Way proper.

Cross the road and turn left along the pavement. After about 100yds bear right on a footpath, signed to Brixton, downhill, soon picking up a narrow path past garden sheds and down steps into mature sycamore woodland, carpeted with bluebells in May. ▶ At the bottom continue through Andron Wood, soon crossing a dog-friendly stile into a huge sweeping field below Hollacombe Wood. Head straight across and over a stile to the right of **Spriddlestone House**, an elegant Grade II listed property. An earlier mansion on this site dated from the time of Henry VI and was home until the 18th century to a branch of the wealthy and influential Fortescue family. The level grassy track ahead gives way to a hedged path, emerging between stone gateposts on to a lane junction in the hamlet of **Spriddlestone**.

This path is steep, and very slippery when wet.

Turn right past pretty Pine Cottage and Little Spriddlestone Barn. Just before the next cottage on the right bear left up steps and over two stiles. Follow the left field edge, with extensive views across the rolling South Hams countryside.

Cross a wooden stile and keep alongside the hedge, soon bearing right across the field to a stile. Keep along the left edge of the next field; cross a stile onto a fenced

Hayfield near Spriddlestone in high summer

path. A metal gate gains a steep flight of steps into beech woodland, above a stream; descend to Brixton Torr, at the head of tidal (and often wet underfoot) **Cofflete Creek**. Cofflete/Brixton Torr Mill once stood nearby, but was demolished in the 1950s. Note the ford and delightful little stone footbridge, almost overwhelmed by modern road surfacing work.

Follow the lane past the bridge, soon passing under a substantial brick bridge.

> The bridge once carried the **Great Western Railway branch line** from Plymouth's Millbay Station to Brixton and Yealmpton, which snaked alongside the creeks of the River Yealm. The line opened in 1898 and closed in 1930, reopening again for six years from 1941 to assist those who had moved out of Plymouth into the countryside during and just after World War II.

Ascend steeply; just before the lane starts to level bear right up steps and cross a stile onto a fenced path, which ends at a stone stile and footpath junction; turn left up the lane to reach the A379 at the west end of **Brixton**. Turn right, then cross the road onto Lodge Lane. Ascend to a crossroads, with views towards Lee Moor china clay works on the southern edge of Dartmoor.

> Dartmoor's **china clay industry** dates from the 1830s, when significant deposits of kaolin – resulting from the decomposition of feldspar in the granite – were

Brixton's war memorial and parish church of St Mary

discovered on Lee Moor. Originally used in the production of porcelain (which is why it is known as 'china' clay), today the bulk of what is quarried is used in paper manufacture and also in the ceramic and pharmaceutical industries. The scarred landscape comes as something of a surprise to those unaware of Dartmoor's sole surviving industry: tin mining ended in the early 20th century, and the last commercial granite quarry, Merrivale, closed in 1997 after 121 years of operation. In the summer of 2014 a new tungsten mining operation started at Hemerdon, just off the moor's southwestern edge.

Turn right; after a few yards turn right through a metal gate and cross the field diagonally left. At the far corner a tight kissing gate leads to a narrow path between houses. Cross the road and follow the footpath ahead, descending steps. Pass a disused building, soon bearing right downhill as signed, on Legion Lane, to meet the A379. Turn left to find St Mary's Church and Mary Green General Store (with coffee shop).

The first mention of a **chapel at Brixton** dates from a 1309 register of Exeter's Bishop Stapleton; the present building originates largely from the late 15th century, with the interior refurbished in the early 19th century. A window in the vestry dates from the 15th century and came from the old Spriddlestone Manor; there is also a Spriddlestone chapel, for the Fortescue family's private worship. There's a rather lovely Victorian lamppost near the church gate, marking Queen Victoria's Diamond Jubilee in 1897.

A community path leads downhill right and alongside the A379 to Riverford Farm Shop at Kitley.

At the General Store bear left up Old Road; cross the next road and bear slightly left along Woodland Drive, through a housing estate; at the end a gate leads into fields. ◄ Head across the field and over a stile at the end. In the next large field bear half left to a woodland corner, then descend steeply into the valley.

Thatched Tapps Lodge, seen across the fields, is one of the lodge gates for 500-year-old **Kitley House**, now a hotel, situated to the south of the A379. The house is thought to have been built in the reign of King Henry VIII by Thomas Pollexfen – whose family lived there until 1710 – and remodelled in the early 19th century by George Stanley Repton, youngest son of celebrated landscape designer Sir Humphrey Repton.

Pass through a gate and cross a stile; at a footpath sign turn to follow the field edge, aiming for a plantation.

At the top turn left, soon bearing right around the edge of the wood. Head across the next field, passing a footpath post. Enjoy sweeping views from the roughly beaten path that descends towards a clump of trees, then bear right at another post. Cross a stile into **Gorlofen Plantation** – with bluebells and wild garlic in May – under sycamore and oak. Descend steps onto a lane.

Turn right to ascend past pretty, thatched, Gothic-style Gorlofen Lodge, another lodge gate for Kitley House. About 200yds after a lane junction, by a gate, turn right over a stile into a field. Turn left to pass a footpath post and continue steeply uphill, crossing a stile into the next field. Turn left; soon pass through the hedge and along the right edge of the next two fields; houses on the edge of **Yealmpton** come into view.

The next gate leads onto a track; follow this to meet a lane, and turn right downhill. Just before Bowden Farm turn right on a footpath, descending steeply. On meeting the A379 turn left to pass The Volunteer pub to gain the crossroads in the middle of the village, with Noss Mayo/ Newton Ferrers signed right.

Yealmpton's colourful village sign

The sprawling village of **Yealmpton** is well served both by transport links (buses to Plymouth and Dartmouth) and places to eat and drink. Market Street Café has a takeaway menu, and hot drinks are available from The Village Stores. Take some time to look around St Bartholomew's Church, completely rebuilt (apart from the tower) between 1849 and 1851 and said by poet Sir John Betjeman to be 'the most amazing Victorian church in Devon'. The screen, pillars and altar stone are all made of Kitley marble, quarried in the parish.

49

STAGE 2
Yealmpton to Ivybridge

Start	Yealmpton, crossroads on the A379 in village centre (SX 579 518)
Finish	Ivybridge, The Watermark, Erme Court (SX 637 562)
Distance	9 miles (14.5km)
Time	4½hrs
Terrain	Rolling fields, wooded valleys, riverside paths
Maps	Explorer OL20 South Devon; Landranger 202 Torbay & South Dartmoor
Refreshments	Crooked Spire pub, Ermington (off route), pubs and cafés in Ivybridge
Public toilets	Ivybridge (Glanvilles Mill car park)
Public transport	For Yealmpton: Plymouth–Dartmouth/Newton Ferrers bus routes; for Ivybridge: mainline railway and bus routes to Exeter, Totnes and Plymouth
Parking	Glanvilles Mill car park and Erme Court car parks (pay & display), Ivybridge
Accommodation	B&B, camping, bunkhouse
Note	Unless planning to visit Ermington, make sure you buy enough food and drink for the day before setting off. There are no other refreshment stops on this stage.

Stage 2 is similar to its predecessor in terms of landscape quality, as field paths and woodland tracks in rolling countryside are followed towards the River Erme, which is then followed on and off north towards Ivybridge on Dartmoor's southern edge. The way passes near the attractive village of Ermington, a handy spot for lunch (via a short detour). Ivybridge has plenty of facilities for walkers and good transport links.

From the crossroads in the centre of **Yealmpton** turn right down Torr Hill, passing Church Lane (access to the church). Join the Newton Ferrers/Noss Mayo road and keep ahead to cross the River Yealm on a footbridge.

STAGE 2 – YEALMPTON TO IVYBRIDGE

Looking at gentle South Hams rivers such as the Yealm and Erme it is hard to imagine them in spate. But Yealmpton and Yealmbridge were badly flooded in July 2012 when more than three inches (over 80mm) of rainfall fell in 24 hours. As early as the 14th century the state of such rivers was a cause for concern when waste material from **Dartmoor's tin-mining industry**, dumped in the moorland streams, clogged up the lower reaches and mouths of many waterways. A book of 1725 records 'marvellous great quantity of sand, gravel, stone, rubble, earth, slime and filth' transported down from moorland tin-streaming works.

Just over the bridge turn left on a pretty riverside path, which eventually bears right to meet the end of a residential road. Bear left along a fenced path. Cross a stile into a field and follow the left edge to cross a stile. Bear right diagonally across the next field; pass through a gap in the hedgebank and along the right edge of the next field. Cross a stone stile and follow a rough green lane, eventually crossing a footbridge into a field. Continue straight on to cross a stile and follow a narrow fenced path past a disused limestone quarry at **Yealmbridge**, now a vehicle storage area. When passing the gates look left to spot a tollhouse on the A379.

The **Yealmbridge tollhouse** dates from 1809. By 1827 all the main roads across the South Hams had been constructed by Turnpike Trusts; the first in the area linked Totnes with Modbury in 1759. The tollhouse keeper would extract a fee from those using

map continues
on page 54

A curious effigy of St Dunstan, Archbishop of Canterbury in the 10th century, set in a South Devon wall

the new road (Sunday churchgoers, coffin bearers and carts carrying building materials were exempt).

The path ends at a lane; turn right uphill to pass a shrine to the renowned St Dunstan, set in the high wall of Dunstone House. The reason for the shrine is unknown: Dunstan was Archbishop of Canterbury from AD960–78,

View north across the fertile rolling fields of the South Hams

and has no confirmed connection with Devon or the hamlet of **Dunstone**. Continue uphill to pass Dunstone Farmhouse.

About 200yds later turn left over a stile by a gate and follow a line of posts across the field. Pass through a small gate and keep along the left field edge. The next gate leads to a path junction on the edge of a huge sloping field, with lovely views towards Dartmoor.

The right of way runs right along the hedge, then left across the top of the field, heading for a solitary post, and then another by an ash tree. Cross the stile ahead, and keep the hedge left. After 250yds bear right across the field (look for a sign in the hedge); cross the next stile and follow the left field edge, dropping downhill. Cross another stile and descend to a lane.

Turn left. ▶ Just past some light industrial units turn right on a little-used lane that descends gently alongside Flete Wood (good bluebells in spring). Where the lane bears 90 degrees right turn left on a hedged track,

Take care: although this appears to be a quiet rural lane, cars speed along here.

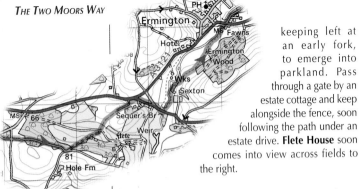

keeping left at an early fork, to emerge into parkland. Pass through a gate by an estate cottage and keep alongside the fence, soon following the path under an estate drive. **Flete House** soon comes into view across fields to the right.

map continues on page 57

Grade I listed **Flete House** – now a retirement 'village' – dates from the 16th century and was heavily remodelled in the late 19th when the castellated towers were added, giving it a distinctly fortified appearance from this distance. Flete, on the banks of the River Erme, was originally a Saxon manor.

The path ascends between banks of sycamore and hazel to pass through two gates, then drops downhill. Where it bears sharp left cross a stile on the right and a field to meet the fast-moving **A379**.

Cross the road to find a stile and field-edge path, protected from the traffic. Cross the A3121 at Hollowcombe Cross, and continue alongside the road over marshy ground, thick with frothy meadowsweet and brilliant yellow flag irises in summer. ◄ Cross a stile and two footbridges; bear right onto the road to cross **Sequer's Bridge**, which sits at the head of the Erme estuary; the river is tidal just to the south of this spot.

Chestnut-coloured South Devon cattle – known locally as 'Orange Elephants' on account of their colour and bulk – graze on the verdant riverside pasture.

Turn left down steps and over a stile, and keep ahead across the riverside meadow. A gate leads into another field; bear left to cross a ditch on slabs. Head up the field, eventually bearing right alongside and then into a coniferous plantation. Ascend to a gate into a field; climb steeply, bearing slightly left to a kissing gate. Head across the next field and through a gate and then stile into a huge field that slopes down towards the river, below **Ermington Wood**.

*Hawthorn in
full bloom near
Sequer's Bridge*

The little village of **Ermington**, seen on the west side of the valley, is renowned for its church's crooked 14th-century spire, its curvature resulting from the use of unseasoned timbers in its construction (not, as local legend would have it, the spire bowing in honour of a particularly beautiful bride and then being unable to straighten up!). When it was struck by lightning in 1856, the chance to straighten the spire was rejected by local parishioners. Western Beacon on Dartmoor's southern edge looms invitingly in the distance.

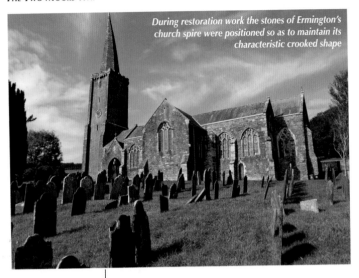

During restoration work the stones of Ermington's church spire were positioned so as to maintain its characteristic crooked shape

Descend diagonally left to the bottom corner of the field to rejoin the Erme. Pass through a succession of gates alongside the river and then a track past buildings at **Fawns**. Pass through a kissing-gate by an open-fronted barn; stone steps and stile lead to the **A3121**.

Turn left with care (no pavement); just before crossing Erme Bridge turn right on a lane signed to Pencuit and Strode House. ◀ Ascend steadily for about a mile, passing under a line of stunning beech trees near **Strode House**.

For Ermington village keep ahead on the A3121 and take the next turn right; at the T-junction turn left for the pub.

Strode House was the primary home of the renowned Strode family from the 13th to 15th centuries. Traces of the former mansion can be discerned in the fabric of the farmhouse today. **Richard Strode**, MP for Plympton in 1512, spent time in Lydford gaol after conviction by the four stannary courts (see Stage 5) for 'conduct subversive of the tinners' liberties'. He had tried to introduce a bill to restrain mining operations near seaports to prevent harbours becoming choked with waste.

As the lane levels ignore a small lane coming in right; almost immediately the lane starts to drop. By the first gate on the left cross a V-stile and descend alongside the right hedge to cross a very high stile in boggy ground at the bottom corner. Cut diagonally left across the next field, to cross a high stone stile on a hedge corner. ▶

Bear left downhill on a field track towards **Thornham Bridge**, which crosses the Erme over to the left. Pass through two open gateways and along the right edge of an old orchard, and the next field. Continue in the same direction to cross hefty stone steps onto a lane on a bend.

Keep ahead to a T-junction at Caton Cross. Turn left; just before **Keaton Bridge** turn right up a track (Cole Lane), soon passing a weir. ▶ Follow the riverside path past a ford, then through a kissing gate into a large meadow. The path runs along its right edge, soon along an avenue of trees. Cross a stile and follow a walled track between fields, then a tarmac drive past a bungalow to meet a road on a bend.

Turn left along the verge, soon picking up a path that parallels the road. Cross the drive that leads to **Cleeve**; a few paces later turn left to walk along the perimeter of playing fields, then alongside the river again to pass the impressive South Devon Tennis Centre and under a road. On meeting the road again turn left to pass under two roads, then follow a tarmac path along the riverbank and past the Leisure Centre, soon picking up signs for the Information Centre. Pass the footbridge to Glanvilles Mill shopping centre; where the Erme bears away left follow the tarmac path ahead, after a few steps bearing left on a walkway between shops to find The Watermark and tourist information centre. If it's open you can ask to sign the Two Moors Way/Devon Coast-to-Coast record book.

Notice how the nature of the landscape becomes more broken up as the southern moor is approached, with smaller, steeper fields and taller, thicker hedges.

However tempting it may look there is no access to the river here.

The River Erme rushes away from the moor at Ivybridge

Ivybridge started life as a hamlet clustered around the 13th-century Ivy Bridge over the River Erme (the inspiration for a painting by JMW Turner and the location for 'The Battle of the Bridge' re-enactment held annually to commemorate a dispute between the villagers of Ivybridge and Ermington). It became a staging post on the London–Plymouth road, and expanded further in the 19th century with the development of mills along the fast-flowing Erme and the coming of the railway in 1848. Bypassed by the A38 in 1973, its population has expanded rapidly and it is one of Devon's less characterful towns, although conveniently situated on the mainline railway and major road links. It is by far the largest town encountered on the Devon Coast to Coast, and comes as something of a surprise after two days' walking through the peaceful South Hams countryside. Walkers can find all facilities here, and there is helpful advice available at the tourist information centre (closed Saturday afternoons and Sundays).

STAGE 3
Ivybridge to Holne

Start	Ivybridge, The Watermark, Erme Court (SX 637 562)
Finish	Holne (SX 706 695)
Distance	13½ miles (21.75km)
Time	7hrs
Terrain	Exposed track; pathless moorland, often wet underfoot
Maps	Explorer OL28 Dartmoor; Landranger 202 Torbay & South Dartmoor; Harvey Map Two Moors Way
Refreshments	The Watermark Café, Ivybridge; The Tradesman's Arms, Scorriton (off route); Holne Village Stores and Tearoom, Church House Inn
Public toilets	None en route
Public transport	For Ivybridge: mainline railway and bus routes to Exeter, Totnes and Plymouth; no public transport to Holne
Parking	Pay & display car parks, Ivybridge; laneside in Holne
Accommodation	B&B, camping
Notes	This section of the route is unsigned, so unless you are competent with map and compass, do not attempt this stage in poor weather. Take all food and drink with you from the start.

This stage is the first on the Two Moors Way: in terms of landscape and walking conditions it is a huge change from the gentle and leafy countryside experienced so far. On leaving Ivybridge, the route immediately encounters barren and lonely moorland, peppered with evidence of Bronze Age activity, and you may well see no sign of human life until Holne. After leaving the trackbed of the old Red Lake Railway (a 6½-mile/10.5km trudge, particularly tough on those rare occasions when the wind is blowing from the north), pathless and, in places, wet ground is crossed until the moor is left at Chalk Ford, roughly two miles from the end of the stage.

Note that the official Two Moors Way signpost by The Watermark states 102 miles to Lynmouth.

◀ Pass to the left of The Watermark and follow the lane to meet Fore Street (town centre and shops left) at New Bridge. Cross over and follow the path alongside the River Erme, passing the 'snail' turbine, a water-driven turbine once used for powering Ivybridge's old corn mill (now the site of Glanvilles Shopping Centre). Follow Two Moors Way signs through riverside gardens to reach Harford Road; keep ahead, passing the older Ivy Bridge, originally a packhorse bridge dating from the 13th century. Continue uphill, soon passing the impressive building that once housed Stowford Paper Mill (closed late 2013).

A rainbow marks the onward route as the moor is reached at last

To the left of the paper mill chimney can be seen the lofty viaduct that carries the main London–Penzance railway line, towering above the wooded Erme valley. The renowned engineer **Isambard Kingdom Brunel** had the first viaduct built on this spot in 1848 to carry the broad gauge track of the South Devon Railway (taken over by the Great

Western Railway in 1876). In the 1890s a granite-and-brick viaduct replaced the original wooden structure, reusing Brunel's pillars; the granite was quarried at Western Beacon, soon passed on the route. Ivybridge's old railway station was situated just west of the viaduct.

Ascend steeply past Ivybridge Community College; at the top cross Cole Lane to reach Stowford Bridge Cross and the Dartmoor National Park boundary. Look out for the official Two Moors Way stone, bearing the opening date: '29th May 1976'.

Cross the railway line via Stowford Bridge and walk up Harford Lane. By **Stowford House** (left) – a former manor house dating from the 16th century – turn right on a public bridleway, soon following the track sharp left and ascending gently to a gate with glorious views ahead over (at last!) open moorland.

Alternative route via Western Beacon

An attractive ridge-top option with far-reaching views can be taken instead of the official route. Once through the gate take the grassy path right – crossing a track en route – to ascend to the top of **Western Beacon**, then turn left (north) along the ridge and continue across cairn-studded **Butterdon Hill**, alongside a stone row. The stone row crosses the Two Moors Way not far from Hangershell Rock; in the 19th century well-attended horse races were held on level ground just to the east of this point. Rejoin the main route below **Hangershell Rock**.

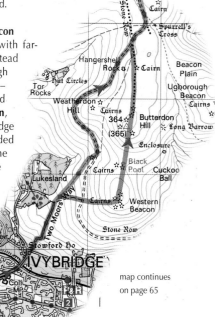

map continues on page 65

61

From the gate, three grassy ways stretch away ahead: follow the bridlepath and bear half right up the central one (north-northeast) towards **Butterdon Hill**, to meet a disused trackbed running along the contours at an MW marker stone, dated 2002. In the distance to the northwest can be seen the white-scarred landscape of the Lee Moor china clay works (see Stage 1), just outside the national park boundary.

Turn left along the track – the old Red Lake Railway – rounding the lower slopes of **Weatherdon Hill**, and passing below **Hangershell Rock**, one of Dartmoor's iconic granite tors, weathered by rain and frost into fantastic shapes. ◄

The alternative route via Western Beacon rejoins the main route here.

Note a line of widely spaced small upright stones crossing the track in a south–north direction: this is one of the moor's longest **stone rows** (restored), running from Butterdon Hill north to the Longstone, a once recumbent standing stone that was re-erected in the 1990s. The longest stone row in the world (over 2 miles long) is found to the northwest on Stall

Heading towards Hangershell Rock

Moor. Restored Spurrell's Cross sits atop the ridge nearby (only the head is original); most such crosses on Dartmoor date from medieval times and mark moorland routes used by local abbeys.

The **Red Lake Railway** was completed in 1910 and officially opened in 1911 in order to exploit remote deposits of china clay at Red Lake and Left Lake Mires. For a decade the line was well used, but by the early 1930s supplies were exhausted, the China Clay Corporation (with offices in Ivybridge) liquidated, and the track was removed. The line ran from the Cantrel works at Bittaford, east of Ivybridge to the Red Lake railhead, 1475ft (450m) above sea level.

Follow the track in a roughly northerly direction to cross **Piles Hill**; the village seen away to the right is South Brent. A long straight stretch is rewarded with increasingly good views over the Erme valley to the left, and the mound of Stalldown Barrow beyond. The next straight section passes below **Three Barrows** (right); look down-valley to spot Piles Copse.

Dartmoor is home to three areas of **upland oak woodland**, remnants of a once-extensive forest cover: Black-a-tor Copse near Meldon Reservoir; Wistman's Wood near Two Bridges; and Piles Copse, here in the Erme valley. Stunted oaks rise out of a bed of granite clitter (boulders), which has protected the trees from destructive grazing by livestock.

After almost 4 miles (6.4km) of steady walking along the track, the monotony is broken as the track bears right to cross a bridge by a spoil heap and water-filled pit at Leftlake Mires, last worked in the 1920s. ▶ The next big sweep east faces **Quickbeam Hill**; disused tinworkings are passed before the next, at **Brown Heath** – where the clay was held in settling tanks before travelling, in suspension, by gravity to the Cantrel works to be processed

On the bend before the bridge, shelter from the wind can be found among the ruins of a building to the right of the track.

The Two Moors Way stone near Red Lake: the onward route crosses the open common

The next section of the route – as far as Chalk Ford – is in places indistinct, and often rough and boggy underfoot.

– brings views north across barren moorland towards the impressive spoil heap at the old Red Lake China Clay Works, where the trackbed ends.

About 100yds after passing the ruins of a stone building (left) – and as the tramway bears left towards Red Lake – look out for a second MW marker stone. ◀ Bear right – now on the Abbot's Way, which is followed to Huntingdon Cross – through a gap in the bank.

The Abbot's Way is so named as it has been suggested monks used it from the 12th century when travelling between Buckfast Abbey and those at Tavistock and Buckland Monachorum, to the west of the moor. It is sometimes known as 'Jobber's Path', a reference to its origins as a packhorse route for yarn jobbers transporting wool across the moor since at least medieval times.

Bear half left up an obvious beaten path, uphill, keeping left of low mounds of china clay spoil. Cross a sunken path – the line of the old Zeal Tor Tramway, a short-lived horse-drawn venture constructed in the mid 19th century to transport peat from Red Lake to naphtha works at Shipley Bridge – at a spot known as **The Crossways**. Cross the brow of the hill, passing to the left of a small stone structure. The path contours left and downhill into the Avon valley; on the hillside opposite note two round enclosures, with 'humps' on the ground between them, remnants of pillow mounds associated with rabbit farming.

Rabbits were farmed across Dartmoor for both fur and food from the mid 13th century to the 1950s. **Huntingdon Warren** is one of 18 warrens set up across the moor; many were established near tinworkings to provide workers with food and skins (see Stage 5). Rabbits were farmed here from around 1800 to the 1930s.

map continues on page 67

65

The more direct – and more obvious – path drops steeply over rough, wet and rocky ground to reach the clapper bridge but is not the official route.

Keep high, parallel to the Avon (or Aune), for a short way to find a tinstreaming gully, then descend to the river. ◄ On the bank turn left upstream to find and cross a 19th-century **clapper bridge**, formed of large granite slabs on low 'piers', a typical feature of the moors of England's southwest, often dating from medieval times and sited – as in this example – close to fords.

As mentioned in the Introduction rainfall totals on the southwest's moors are relatively high. Stream levels can rise (and fall) remarkably fast, and thus stream crossings (where there is no bridge) can become difficult. The Western Wella Brook, which has to be crossed a little way on near Huntingdon Cross, is a typical example: the following two alternative paths lead to a bridge over the brook a short way upstream, from where the main route may be rejoined between Hickaton Hill and Pupers Hill.

First high-water variant

This option – which enjoys good views downriver towards the Avon reservoir, and gains a close look at the

The Avon is crossed via a clapper bridge

remains of Huntingdon Warren – may be taken after crossing the **clapper bridge**, and it offers an easier alternative to the second high-water variant.

From the bridge bear half-right to cross the lower slopes of **Huntingdon Warren** in a northeasterly direction, ascending quite steeply and passing below the summit before descending alongside walled enclosures near the site of the old Warren House. Pick up a track running east from the settlement and turn right across the Western Walla Brook. ▸ Follow a sunken track, which climbs along the southern flank of **Pupers Hill**. The 'tank'-shaped tor seen on the hilltop right is Eastern White Barrow, the southernmost point on the ancient Forest boundary.

The track starts to descend, with views ahead across the green fields of south Devon as far as the Teign estuary and the sea beyond. Reach a path crossing the track, and soon rejoin the 'official' main route, which approaches from the right via an old boundary bank.

Once across the **clapper bridge** the main route turns right and takes a path that follows the contours about 100yds away from the river, soon becoming indistinct. The ground is boggy and difficult in places; ascend slightly to avoid the worst ground. On reaching a wall look towards the Avon to find **Huntingdon Cross**, a 16th-century Forest of Dartmoor boundary marker. If the Western Wella Brook, on the opposite side of the wall, is in spate (as it frequently is), take the second high-water variant.

map continues
on page 70

The second high-water variant joins up from the south here.

Second high-water variant
Turn left upstream, clambering over rough and wet ground to meet field walls at **Huntingdon Warren** and the former site of Warren House.

> Look out for a ruined building on the east bank of the brook. This is the site of **Keble Martin's Chapel**, built in 1909 by brothers – and devout Christians – Jack and William Keble Martin (the latter perhaps best known as a wildflower artist and author of *The Concise British Flora in Colour*). The chapel – which never had a roof – is sited at grid reference 666 666 (the biblical number of 'the beast'). A curious coincidence, perhaps…

Stay alongside fields, crossing streams as required, to meet a track and bridge, joining the first high-water variant.

For the main route from Huntingdon Cross, ford the Western Wella Brook (no bridge). Follow the path ahead over **Hickaton Hill**, keeping to the left of an enclosure (settlement). Cross level ground (Pupers Hill left) to meet a track by a low boundary bank and turn right, downhill. ◄

The high-water variants join from the left here.

A short distance from the junction reach a fork in the track – the tower of Buckfast Abbey can be seen in the distance ahead – take the left path, which contours across **Buckfastleigh Moor**, dropping gently through gorse and scattered hawthorn trees and crossing a leat, or water channel, en route.

Do not stray too far to the left; keep in a roughly northeasterly direction, continually descending, to pick up an obvious path that descends into the wooded valley to meet the River Mardle at **Chalk Ford**. Cross the footbridge, then follow the track uphill via a gate, passing through another at the hilltop. Descend for over a mile – keeping left at a T-junction – to reach another T-junction in **Scorriton**. ◄ Turn right; 50yds later turn left by the war memorial and descend to a T-junction; turn left to cross Holy Brook bridge. The Holy Brook was originally known

Turn left here for The Tradesman's Arms.

Walkers leaving the route of the Two Moors Way on Buckfastleigh Moor

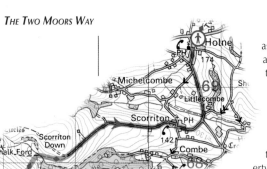

as the Northbrooke and flows into the River Dart at Buckfast Abbey, where at one time it formed one of the boundaries of the Abbey property. Where the lane bears right keep ahead past an Elizabeth II Golden Jubilee stone and climb very steeply up a hedged green lane: a bit of a killer at the end of a long day!

Eventually the green lane levels and meets a lane; keep ahead, then turn right into the little village of **Holne**. Pass the Community Stores and Tearoom and the 14th-century church of St Mary the Virgin, to find the Church House Inn – originally built as the priest's house – in the village centre.

The peaceful village of **Holne** (the name means simply 'holly') occupies a sheltered spot to the east of Holne Moor, between the valleys of the Holy Brook and the River Dart. The novelist and historian Charles Kingsley, author of *The Water Babies* and *Westward Ho!*, was born in the vicarage in 1819. The family later moved to Clovelly on the north Devon coast. Today the village is justifiably proud of its community shop, one of many to have sprung up around the county in the last 10 years or so, and perfectly situated to supply the needs of weary walkers.

STAGE 4

Holne to Dunstone Down

Start	Holne, crossroads in village centre (SX 706 695)
Finish	Dunstone Down, crossroads on southern end of Hamel Down (SX 704 759)
Alternative Finish	Widecombe-in-the-Moor, village green (SX 718 768)
Distance	7¼ miles (11.75km); or 9 miles (14.5km)
Time	4hrs; or 4½ hrs
Terrain	Steep-sided river valleys and woodland; good tracks, paths and lanes
Maps	Explorer OL28 Dartmoor; Landranger 202 Torbay & South Dartmoor, 191 Okehampton & North Dartmoor; Harvey Map Two Moors Way
Refreshments	Holne Village Stores and Tearoom, Church House Inn; cafés and pubs in Widecombe
Public toilets	Widecombe
Public transport	None available
Parking	Laneside in Holne and on Dunstone Down; pay & display in Widecombe (alternative finish)
Accommodation	B&B, bunkhouse
Note	Stock up with food and drink before setting out; there are no other opportunities on this stage (apart from ice cream vans at New Bridge and Bel Tor Corner car parks in season).

A bit of light relief in terms of landscape after the bleak moorland expanse encountered on Stage 3, and a much shorter day – but one that is still relatively taxing, with a succession of descents and ascents as the route negotiates the steep-sided Dart valley, where the river has cut deeply into the softer rocks below the granite edge. The stage ends with a steady climb from the pretty West Webburn river onto the southern slopes of Hamel Down. An alternative finish to find facilities in Widecombe-in-the-Moor may be necessary at the end of the day.

The Dart, one of Dartmoor's loveliest rivers

With the Church House Inn left keep ahead at the crossroads and ascend to a T-junction (Butts Cross). Turn left; after 50yds turn right through a small gate along a fenced path, with lovely views ahead to blocky Buckland Beacon and the steep-sided wooded Dart valley.

Drop gently to cross a stile into a field. Continue to descend in the same direction, enjoying good views up the steep-sided Dart valley below Bench Tor; in the third field bear right on a well-trodden path that descends towards Cleave Wood. The lovely woodland path drops to meet a track; keep ahead, signed Newbridge, alongside the rushing waters of the River Dart, keeping an eye out for the charismatic dipper. Keep left at a fork, soon meeting the road via a gate.

Turn left to cross narrow 15th-century **New Bridge**; immediately turn left again, then sharp left

map continues
on page 76

Sharp Tor overlooks the upper Dart valley

The bulk of Hamel Down as seen from the descent to Locksgate Cross

down steps onto the rocky riverbank, and pass under the bridge. ▶

If the river is too high to allow access, follow the road ahead then along the valley to pick up the official route again at Deeper Marsh.

On meeting the river you may notice a level platform of rock at the water's edge. Known as 'The Slab' this is the launching spot for kayakers and canoeists wishing to tackle 'The Loop', one of the most popular stretches of whitewater in England, and which finishes 3 miles (4.8km) downstream at Holne Bridge.

Follow the rooty and uneven riverside path, which rises high above the water, soon descending back towards the river from a path junction. Skirt the level sward at Deeper Marsh, a popular spot with picnickers (and bathers) in good weather. Stay alongside the river until it loops sharply away towards Buckland Bridge, and bear left to meet the road. Cross over and ascend the steep unsigned woodland path, which zigzags up the valley side before running left along the top of the woods, ascending gently (through a forest of bracken in high summer) to pass the scattered outcrops leading to **Leigh Tor**. After the tor keep the hedge on the right to meet the road.

From Leigh Tor there are good views of Buckland-in-the-Moor church and beacon. The clock face of St Peter's Church is unusual in that the numbers have been replaced with letters spelling out MY DEAR MOTHER and there is a memorial in the churchyard to William Pollexfen Bastard (died 1915), formerly of Kitley, latterly resident at Buckland Court. Buckland Beacon is famous for the **Ten Commandments Stones**, inscribed into the granite in 1928 on the orders of the then Lord of Buckland Manor, William Whitley.

Cross the road and follow a grassy path ahead to cross a minor road. Bear left along a track, heading for an abandoned quarry, before which turn right uphill to reach a broad and level track, and turn left to follow it northwest to skirt **Aish Tor**.

On Dr Blackall's Drive, heading towards Mel Tor

Scenic carriageways were popular in the 19th century, and in the 1870s the resident of nearby 17th-century Spitchwick Manor, Dr Joseph Blackall, had one laid out for his wife's benefit after she could no longer walk on the moor. Today **Dr Blackall's Drive**, running high above the Dart, provides a convenient walking route with spectacular views over the valley to craggy Bench Tor and as far as the radio mast on North Hessary Tor above Princetown.

Beautiful at any time of year, this stretch is particularly lovely in late summer when the slopes are covered with purple ling and bell heather, interspersed with the gold flowers of Western gorse; and in autumn the colours of the predominantly oak woodland are glorious.

Follow the drive (rocky underfoot) away from the valley – along a walled drift lane – and past well-preserved Bronze Age hut circles near **Mel Tor**. Where the wall bears away

90 degrees right follow it to the parking area at **Bel Tor Corner**. ▶ Cross the B3357 with care. Follow the obvious path ahead, soon bearing left, with wonderful views of the Hamel Down ridge and the onward route ahead. At a fork bear right, downhill, to pass to the left of a walled enclosure at Primm Cottage. Follow grassy paths ahead through bracken and stands of gorse to meet a lane.

Turn right downhill over Locksgate Cross and descend steeply to reach the little ford at **Ponsworthy** (Forder Bridge).

Ponsworthy comprises just a few attractive granite houses and farms, mostly clustered around Ponsworthy Bridge along the lane to the left of the ford. The renovated cottages by the ford used to include the smithy. Local legend has it that sparks flew when the Devil rode his horse full tilt across the narrow bridge in 1638 en route from the inn at Poundsgate to Widecombe to settle a bet with one Jan Reynolds (see Stage 5).

During the holiday season there is usually an ice-cream van in the car park.

Picture-postcard cottages at Forder Bridge, Ponsworthy

Do not cross the ford but turn left on a narrow footpath that follows the river for about a mile. This is a delightful path: riverside meadows near the start are thick with early purple orchids, sorrel and hemp agrimony in early summer; the woodland is carpeted with bluebells and then ransoms in May. Cross the river on a footbridge to pass between cottage gardens at **Jordan Mill**, to meet a lane. Follow the lane steeply uphill to pass Drywell Farm, keeping straight on at the crossroads marked by Drywell Cross. Descend past lovely Dockwell Farm, then ascend steeply towards Hamel Down. Look out for a small gate on the left signed to Hutholes.

Divert from the route to visit **Hutholes**, a medieval settlement dating from before 1350, at which time it was abandoned for some reason, possibly wiped out by the Black Death or deteriorating climatic conditions. The wall remnants indicate two longhouses and various agricultural structures. Local knowledge has it that stone from the buildings was taken to build Jordan Manor, passed a mile before.

Continue up the lane for 150yds to reach a crossroads on the edge of Dunstone Down at the southern end of Hamel Down.

History relates that the village lengthman and council workmen annually recut two crosses in the turf here, near the boundaries of Widecombe Town, Blackslade and Dunstone, and Jordan manors.

Alternative finish at Widecombe-in-the-Moor

For Widecombe head along the lane, soon passing the Two Crosses car park, identified by an engraved stone placed at the spot in 2008 to reinstate the site's correct name. ◄ Drop down steeply **Southcombe Hill** to reach a T-junction. Turn left to pass the village school – Widecombe Fair is held in the field to the right – and reach The Old Inn and St Pancras Church.

Widecombe-in-the-Moor is one of Dartmoor's honeypot villages and it is enormously popular with coach parties and day-trippers. The parish church of St Pancras is known as the 'Cathedral of the Moor' on account of its impressively high tower. This was the site of a disaster in October 1638 when it was struck by lightning; at least six people were killed. Local legends link the event with the work of the Devil but recent research attributes 'The Great Thunderstorm' to an earthquake and associated ball lightning. Widecombe's annual September fair – and the story of Tom Cobley and his grey mare – is a world-famous event, and the village provides good facilities for walkers.

The medieval settlement of Hutholes lies just off the route

STAGE 5
Dunstone Down to Chagford Bridge

Start	Dunstone Down, crossroads on southern end of Hamel Down (SX 704 759)
Alternative Start	Widecombe-in-the-Moor, village green (SX 718 768)
Finish	Chagford Bridge (SX 694 880)
Distance	9½ miles (15.25km)
Time	5½hrs
Terrain	Open moorland, undulating field paths and woodland tracks; lanes and field paths (often wet) on alternative start from Widecombe; steep descent to Chagford Bridge
Maps	Explorer OL28 Dartmoor; Landranger 191 Okehampton & North Dartmoor; Harvey Map Two Moors Way
Refreshments	Warren House Inn (off route), Chagford (off route)
Public toilets	Chagford (off route)
Public transport	For Chagford: limited bus service to Okehampton, Exeter and Newton Abbot (via Moretonhampstead)
Parking	Parking areas on Dunstone Down; pay & display in Widecombe (alternative start); laneside near Chagford Bridge (limited); pay & display in Chagford (off route)
Accommodation	B&B
Notes	The moorland section of this stage is unsigned. In bad weather and poor visibility walkers are advised to follow Stage 5A. Stock up with food and drink before setting off.

Extremely varied in terms of landscape, this stage offers 360-degree views along the Hamel Down ridge and visits one of Dartmoor's best-preserved Bronze Age sites at Grimspound as well as an impressive double stone row on Chagford Common. Undulating field paths and woodland tracks – including a stretch of the historic Mariner's Way – are followed, before the route finally drops steeply into the Teign valley just to the west of the pretty little town of Chagford. Before the halfway stage a detour may be made to the famous Warren House Inn for refreshment.

From the crossroads there is a choice of paths for the first half mile of the route. The suggested variant (giving lovely views over Widecombe and the East Webburn valley) is a little easier to follow, but the main route is preferred by both the Ordnance Survey and Harvey maps.

Easier variant
From the crossroads head along the lane to reach a parking area on the left at the top of the hill, at which point turn left (signed) on a broad grassy track and head north across the down. The path meets a wall corner and continues alongside it, rejoining the main route as it approaches from the left.

For the main route, bear half-left from the edge of the down, heading in a north-northeasterly direction and climbing gently. Pick your way across rough ground and through low-growing gorse on the early stages, and eventually find a broad path that runs uphill towards the **Hamel Down** ridge: the well-trodden onward path can be seen ahead. The views improve with every step: to the left from Bellever Tor to the Littaford/Longaford ridge, then east to Fernworthy Forest and the Warren House, the isolated white building seen in the distance. A granite shelf is passed, beyond which the path drops to meet a track running alongside a granite wall, where the variant rejoins the main route.

**Rejoining the main route
from Widecombe**
Those who overnighted in **Widecombe** can rejoin the main route either by retracing their steps to the end-point of Stage 4 on Dunstone Down, or by taking the Natsworthy lane from the village green. Turn left at the first narrow lane and ascend steeply to meet the Two Moors Way on the lower slopes of Hamel Down.

Turn left to reach a wall corner and follow the main path (one of four) uphill, ascending steadily.

The Hamel Down ridge is threaded with paths, many of which bear no relation to those marked on the OS map. It is also one of the best places in the area for practising **tor identification**! From left to right over the West Webburn valley (east): Honeybag, Chinkwell, Bel, Bonehill Rocks, Haytor and Low Man, Top Tor, Pil Tor and Rippon Tor, with Tunhill Rocks below, on the slopes of Blackslade Down.

map continues
on page 84

The path passes an unnamed tor and bears half left to reach **Hameldown Beacon** and cairn, set against a drystone wall. The stones marking several of the barrows along the ridge were erected in the mid 19th century by the Duke of Somerset, then Lord of Natsworthy Manor, and bear his initials.

Continue alongside the wall to pass **Two Burrows** (from 'barrow': a burial mound) at the next wall corner, and continue along the ridge-top path. Some of these ridge-top Bronze Age barrows were excavated in the 19th century and were found, uniquely on Dartmoor, to be of the Wessex culture.

Look east again to see Easdon Tor, Hunter's Tor and Hayne Down. Look carefully and you can spot **Bowerman's Nose**, a 40-foot (12.25m) stack of granite on the northern flank of Hayne Down. Bowerman is said to be an 11th-century hunter who disturbed a coven of witches. In revenge they encased him – and his hounds, resulting in the naming of nearby Hound Tor – in stone.

Pass **Single Burrow** (excavations here have revealed the bronze blade and

Haytor Rocks, one of the national park's 'honeypot' sites

amber pommel of a dagger). At **Broad Burrow** the path splits. ▶ Take the path that sets off from the earthwork itself and keeps to the top of the ridge.

> The path bearing right here leads, after a short distance, to a **World War II memorial** to four RAF airmen, killed when their plane crashed at this spot in 1941. They had been returning from operations in France and it is thought that their wireless failed at the same time they encountered thick cloud over the moor. The pilot's mother had the memorial erected the following year, and every Armistice Day poppies are placed at the base of the stone.

Keep straight on towards the cairn and trig point on **Hameldown Tor**, the highest point on the ridge at 1736ft (529m). **Hameldown Cross**, passed en route to the left, is one of the less well-preserved examples of its type on Dartmoor. The village that comes into view away to the right, its church tower prominent, is Moretonhampstead, known as the 'gateway to the High Moor'.

Do not stay on the path you have been following, which bears off east and eventually drops off the ridge.

map continues
on page 89

*The enclosing wall
at Grimspound is
instantly identifiable,
as is the onward path
to Hookney Tor*

From Hameldown
Tor take a good look at the large
stone enclosure in the saddle below. This is
the 4-acre (1.6ha) Bronze Age settlement of **Grimspound**,
thought by many to be Dartmoor's finest prehistoric site.

Grimspound dates from around 1300BC. The wide
(possibly double) enclosure wall once held two
dozen buildings, mainly hut circles (round houses).
Entry from the Hameldown Tor side is via a large,

paved gateway. The site was partially restored after extensive examination in the late 19th century when it came to the attention of the Dartmoor Exploration Committee. Archive photos reveal the partial reconstruction of one hut circle at the centre of the site, including the curved porch, giving protection against the worst Dartmoor weather.

Descend towards the settlement. ▶ The official route of the Two Moors Way skirts the left-hand wall, but it is worth entering the enclosure for a closer look around. On the far side cross the Grimslake stream and take the rough path that ascends steadily to pass between the two main outcrops of **Hookney Tor** then turn right, passing to the right of a third outcrop, then bear left on a broad grassy path to pass between granite gateposts in a tumbledown wall and meet a three-way path junction.

Take the middle path, which bears left and descends to meet a minor road. Cross over and follow the broad path ahead across frequently damp ground.

The building below the path, at the head of the Challacombe valley, is **Headland Warren Farm**. The house dates from at least the 15th century and in the early 19th century housed the Birch Tor Inn, according to William Crossing's guide to Dartmoor (see Appendix E). Rabbits were farmed in a purpose-built warren here to supply miners at the nearby Vitifer and Birch Tor and Golden Dagger mines. Below the Warren House Inn the ground is corrugated as a result of intensive tin-mining activity in the 19th and early 20th centuries; Golden Dagger, the last surviving mine here, closed in 1930.

The path rises around the northern flank of **Birch Tor** (out of sight), with increasingly good views towards Dartmoor's highest ground in the northwest corner of the granite plateau. Descend towards the **B3212** transmoor road, soon bearing right to reach a small car park by **Bennett's Cross**.

Take great care on the way down to Grimspound: the path is extremely rocky.

The heather-covered openworks near Bennett's Cross illustrate Dartmoor's long history of tin-mining activity

Bennett's Cross dates from the 13th century and is thought to have been later named for a 16th-century miner. The cross marks the line of the original track across the moor and has also been used as a parish boundary marker (Chagford and North Bovey parishes) and as a boundary marker for Headland Warren and Vitifer Mine (which is why the initials WB – Warren Bounds – are carved into it).

MAP NOTE

The next section of the Two Moors Way from Bennett's Cross over the southern part of Chagford Common to Yardworthy (where the alternative valley route rejoins the main path) is marked as 'Undefined' on the 1:25,000 OS map, but there is a fairly clear path – avoiding the dampest ground – for most of the way.

Walk across the road to pick up a broad grassy path bearing half-left (west) across the common. The path drops through rough ground (workings at the old

Bushdown Mine) then skirts the head of the Hurston Water valley, alongside a grass-banked disused leat. Head towards the ridge (**Hurston Ridge**) to meet a path at right angles.

A short way down the path to the left lies the **Warren House Inn**. This historic and isolated building – where miners once slaked their thirst – sits alone on the transmoor road and is steeped in legend. It is said that the fire in one of the pub's two hearths has not gone out since 1845, when a shovelful of smouldering peat from the fire at the New Inn (long since gone) across the road, was carried into the building. Keep an eye out for the resident ghost: William Stephens, publican, who shot himself behind the bar in 1929.

The inn overlooks some granite enclosures on the slopes of Birch Tor known as the Devil's Playing Cards, or Four Aces. Legend has it that a young local tin miner named Jan Reynolds made a deal with the Devil that specified that, in return for giving Jan good luck, the Devil could, in seven years' time, claim one of his possessions. Jan made a fortune at cards but when the time came to hand over his due he ran from the Devil, and threw his cards away, and the aces turned to stone.

Turn right and follow the clear path in a northerly direction across **Chagford Common**, above the valley of the Hurston Water. To the left can be seen the dark conifers of Fernworthy Forest, the largest on Dartmoor.

There were once three farms at **Fernworthy**, referred to in the 17th century as 'the village'. The forest was planted from 1919 to 1936, initially to replenish timber supplies after World War I, but the trees also served to enhance the scenic qualities of the reservoir, constructed between 1936 and 1942 in response to the growing demand for water from the Torbay area.

The prehistoric double stone row on Hurston ridge

The path becomes more distinct along the ridge, with views towards blocky Kestor Rock on the northern end of the common. The tor – like many others – is linked with all manner of mysterious stories.

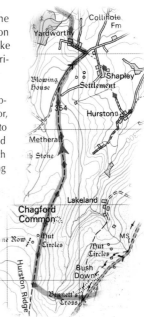

Kestor Rock holds what is thought to be the deepest natural rock basin on any tor on the moor, filled with rainwater and at one time fenced off to prevent sheep from drowning. Victorian legend holds that in the past the basin was used to catch the blood from unfortunates sacrificed during Druidic rites.

Divert off the path to the left to visit the tall standing stone (or menhir) at the top of what is one of the longest and best-preserved double stone rows on Dartmoor: 49 pairs of stones running downhill to a terminating slab. Continue across uneven ground in a northerly direction, keeping to the right of the small valley of the Metherall Brook and aiming for a hedgebank corner by hawthorns. Follow the hedgebank to meet the lane to Fernworthy, descending through a gate by a cattle grid.

About 100yds later turn left on the Mariner's Way/ Two Moors Way signed to Teigncombe and Gidleigh. ▶

map continues on page 90

The alternative route along the Natsworthy valley via Heathercombe, Lettaford and Jurston joins from the right here.

In medieval times a walking route between the north and south coasts was developed in tandem with the growth of Bideford and Dartmouth, enabling sailors to travel between the two ports in search of work. The **Mariner's Way** reached the peak of its popularity in the 18th century, and there are records of alms being given to travelling sailors in Gidleigh church in the mid 1700s. Only this section, keeping to lower ground on the eastern flank of Dartmoor, can be traced with any confidence today.

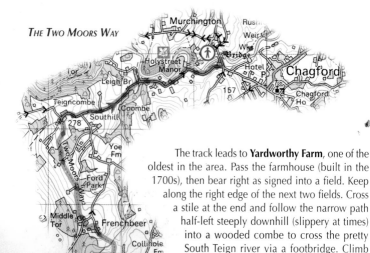

The track leads to **Yardworthy Farm**, one of the oldest in the area. Pass the farmhouse (built in the 1700s), then bear right as signed into a field. Keep along the right edge of the next two fields. Cross a stile at the end and follow the narrow path half-left steeply downhill (slippery at times) into a wooded combe to cross the pretty South Teign river via a footbridge. Climb very steeply out of the valley, with increasingly good views to Meldon Hill to the right.

At the top follow a track alongside a boundary wall at Teignworthy. Pass through a gate between houses and along a track between high hedgebanks. By high gates bear left along a level path, following the wall.

The next section of the route, through a succession of small fields and patches of woodland to Teigncombe, is well signed.

The path ends at a gate; keep ahead between farm buildings to reach a lane at **Great Frenchbeer**. ◀ Cross the lane and go through a gate, then follow the fence below a wooden chalet. The lovely shaded woodland path leads through a gate into an area of scattered hazel trees and bracken, with increasingly good views over the valley of the South Teign river to the right. Follow the clearly signed path across stiles, through gates and fields and along sections of boardwalk over marshy ground, eventually crossing a small footbridge. Continue along the top edge of the next field, bearing left over a small stream at the end and through to gates to reach the lane at **Teigncombe**. ◀

The Mariner's Way keeps straight on towards Gidleigh.

Turn right down the track to reach a tarmac lane on a bend. Keep ahead; where the lane bears sharp right keep straight ahead on a narrower one that degenerates to a track at the gates to Northill and descends steeply to meet a lane to Gidleigh Park hotel.

Bear right, downhill, to cross **Leigh Bridge** over the South Teign, just above the confluence of North and South Teign rivers. This quiet lane passes listed **Holystreet Manor** – dating from the late 16th century, extensively rebuilt in the early 20th, and with a chapel dedicated to St Boniface – and later the kennels of the Mid Devon Hunt, to reach Factory Cross (note the ruined woollen mill on the left). At times there is a cupboard on the grass verge opposite offering snacks and drinks, with an honesty box for payment. ▶ Turn left to pass Corner Cottage and then cross the River Teign via medieval **Chagford Bridge**, to reach the end of Stage 5. The name 'Chagford' comes from the description of the original river crossing here, *chag* being an old dialect word for 'gorse'.

Chagford lies under a mile to the right, up a steep hill.

Chagford is one of Dartmoor's prettiest small towns, with a wealth of independent shops and two extraordinary labyrinthine general stores, Webbens and Bowdens, side-by-side on The Square. There are also plenty of places to grab a bite to eat.

In 1305 Chagford was confirmed by Edward I as one of the four Dartmoor stannary towns (along with Ashburton, Tavistock and later Plympton) where tin was brought for assaying and taxation. In the mid 17th century its fortunes were boosted by the local woollen industry. The octagonal 'Pepperpot' in The Square was built in 1862 by the Rev George Hayter Hames, who also funded various improvements such as a proper water supply and the installation of gas. Opposite The Three Crowns inn stands the 15th-century church of St Michael the Archangel, where Mary Whiddon was shot immediately after her wedding in 1641.

STAGE 5A
Dunstone Down to Chagford Bridge (low-level route)

Start	Dunstone Down, crossroads on southern end of Hamel Down (SX 704 759)
Alternative Start	Widecombe-in-the-Moor, village green (SX 718 768)
Finish	Chagford Bridge (SX 694 880)
Distance	11 miles (17.7km)
Time	6hrs
Terrain	Quiet lanes, tracks and field paths, often wet
Maps	Explorer OL28 Dartmoor; Landranger 191 Okehampton & North Dartmoor; Harvey Map Two Moors Way
Refreshments	Chagford (off route)
Public toilets	Chagford (off route)
Public transport	For Chagford: limited bus service to Okehampton, Exeter and Newton Abbot (via Moretonhampstead)
Parking	Parking areas on Dunstone Down; pay & display in Widecombe (alternative start); laneside near Chagford Bridge (limited); pay & display in Chagford (off route)
Accommodation	B&B
Notes	Stock up with food and drink before setting off.

Although devotees will want to stick to the 'proper' route of the Two Moors Way along the Hamel Down ridge, you may be unlucky and reach this section on one of those frustrating 'Dartmoor days' when somehow dense mist, driving rain and strong winds manage to combine. If you're on a tight schedule and so cannot afford a rest day – and need to make it to your pre-booked accommodation further along the route – you may wish to cut your losses and take the alternative low-level route along the Natsworthy valley, which eventually rejoins the main route north of Chagford Common. Distance and timing are similar, although the valley route involves a number of stile crossings and some boggy stretches. Should conditions improve, there is an option for rejoining the main route from Natsworthy Gate.

Honeybag and Chinkwell tors stand above the valley of the East Webburn, along which the low-level route from Widecombe runs

From the crossroads head along the lane to pass a parking area on the left at the top of the hill. Follow the lane steeply down Southcombe Hill to reach a T-junction and turn left along the lane into the village.

On the edge of the lovely oval village green in **Widecombe** – with lofty horse chestnut and beech trees and handy iron seats – bear left along the lane signed to

Widecombe-in-the-Moor village sign featuring the famous 'Uncle Tom Cobley'

A path soon passed on the left links with the main Two Moors Way route on the southern slopes of Hamel Down.

Natsworthy. ◄ Follow this quiet lane, climbing steadily, soon crossing a cattle grid. After 2 miles (3.2km) follow a signed path through a gate on the right to cut through fields briefly and regain the lane. Continue uphill to pass **Natsworthy Manor**. Around 2½ miles (4km) from the village green reach Natsworthy Gate. Turn left through the gate to reach a path junction.

> The bridlepath seen a few paces up the lane to the right leads to **Jay's Grave**, embedded in local folklore. A simple earth grave with a small granite headstone marks the resting place of Kitty Jay, a local girl who committed suicide when her lover, the son of a wealthy landowner, refused to marry her when she fell pregnant. It is said that the grave is always adorned with fresh flowers, placed there by an unknown hand. Unfortunately today the flowers are often joined by all manner of inappropriate detritus.

Link back to the main route
If the cloud has lifted and you want to pick up the main route again keep ahead at the signpost, signed 'Firth Bridge 1¼ miles' on a broad grassy way. Keep left at the first fork and straight on at the second, crossing the saddle, to reach **Grimspound** and pick up the main route by turning right and ascending to **Hookney Tor**.

Ongoing felling and restoration work in the woodland may involve diversions from the route, but these are always clearly marked.

From the junction turn right on a bridlepath, which passes through Heathercombe Woodlands, now on the route of the Mariner's Way (see Stage 5), which is followed from here to Teigncombe on the Two Moors Way en route to Chagford. ◄

Follow the waymarked path through the woods to meet a path junction at the historic settlement of **Heathercombe**.

> **South and North Heathercombe** are classic examples of Dartmoor longhouses built in the late 15th/early 16th centuries, when farming was supplemented by tin-streaming (a process whereby

heavier tin-bearing ore is separated from lighter silts and sands using water) in Heathercombe Burn. In summer visitors are invited to walk the Heathercombe Sculpture Trail, explore the woodland gardens and have tea at South Heathercombe.

Cross the lane and follow the path to the right of Higher Heathercombe, through a gate and along the left field edge to enter woodland. Bear right at the path junction (look for small yellow arrows) and continue along the edge of the trees. Follow arrows left and then right along a grassy ride, to cross a ladderstile by a gate.

Cross the field, and bear half left across the next, aiming to the right of buildings at **Kendon**. Cross the lane, and head straight across the field; cross the next field, negotiating a granite slab bridge, then bear right to walk alongside a restored hedgebank. Cross two stiles and follow the path uphill by a rough beech hedgebank.

Keep along the top left edge of the next field, then down a hedged track towards the hamlet of **Lower Hookner**. After 75yds bear

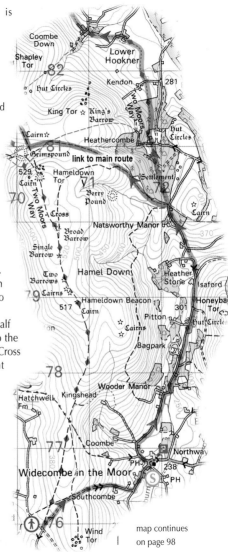

link to main route

map continues on page 98

The fields from here to West Coombe are usually very wet underfoot.

left up steps, then bear half-right towards a stile in the hedge. Pass a footpath post and to the right of a huge beech tree to emerge via a small gate onto a track opposite a house.

Turn left, then right through the next big gate into damp fields. ◄ Turn left along the hedgebank; in the next field bear half-right; in the next keep straight ahead. Bear half-right across the fourth field and over a high stile into scrubby woodland. Look for a yellow splodge on a tree, which indicates an awkward descent down granite steps and across a stream to reach the back of the unrestored longhouse at West Coombe. Pass below the shippon (cattle shed) end to reach a footpath junction.

Cross the track and pass through the gates of the farmhouse opposite, signed to Moor Gate. Continue along a hedgebanked track (often muddy) and into a field, bearing slightly right to a gate in the next hedgebank. Cross the next field to find a footpath post by the stream. Cross over (no bridge) and follow the path through a woodland strip and over a ladderstile. Follow yellow splodges through the trees to emerge into a field; bear left uphill to a gate. Follow the right field edge towards **Moorgate** house, turning right and then left before reaching the building. Keep along the left edge of the next field, then follow the drive to meet the **B3212**.

Cross with care, turning right to cross a stile (Mariner's Way to Lettaford). Bear right towards a gate at the end of the field, then drop alongside the left hedge to pass through a gate and cross a stream. Bear half-right across the next field and continue in the same direction across the next. Cross the next narrow field then bear half-right towards buildings at **Lettaford**. Follow the waymarked path to the left of the buildings, soon bearing right to a path junction.

The hamlet of **Lettaford** is of great historic interest. Records of habitation go back to pre-1300; the three farmhouses seen today were all originally 16th-century longhouses. The lower end of Higher Lettaford was rebuilt by the two Misses

Pynsent around 1840, who may have run a small Noncomformist school here. They were also responsible for the building of the simple chapel in 1866.

At the junction you will encounter a near-perfect example of a Dartmoor longhouse.

Dartmoor has a greater concentration of **longhouses** than anywhere else in England. Sanders, at Lettaford, dates from around AD1500 and still has the usual plan of an inner room, hall, cross-passage and unrestored shippon (byre at the lower end), with a substantial porch covering the entrance for both livestock and people. Longhouses were built tucked into sheltered hollows as protection against the weather and Sanders is made out of huge blocks of worked granite. This particular longhouse was used as a labourer's cottage for generations, and so avoided damaging restoration work.

The extraordinary and beautiful longhouse, 'Sanders', at Lettaford

Turn left past the longhouse, following the track left at Rockmead. High fences denote the site of an old scrapyard. Cross a stream; about 150yds before reaching the lane at **Jurston** bear left uphill across grass towards the old farmhouse. Turn left on the lane; by a stone building turn right (signed to Hurston). Keep along the right edge of four fields, crossing stiles as you go. In the last field pass a memorial bench and descend towards farm buildings at Lingcombe, dropping down steps onto a track.

Turn left past dilapidated buildings; at a sign turn right to pass behind the farmhouse and follow the path (very wet underfoot) through woodland, crossing three streams, to reach a lane. Turn left, signed 'Yardworthy'. At the entrance to **Higher Hurston** take the right fork uphill to pass beautiful Lower Hurston Farm and reach a path junction.

Turn right through two gates; follow the hedge-banked track, and along the right edge of the next field. Turn right through the next gate, immediately left along the hedgebank and through a muddy gateway. Cross a stream in the field corner (very wet) and a stile. Bear slightly right and through a signed gate; follow the hedge towards a bungalow; cross two stiles and keep along the left field edge. Go through a gate and immediately left over a stile to reach buildings at **Shapley**. Bear right, then by a large barn turn left through a gate. Turn right down the farm drive.

map continues
on page 100

98

After about 200yds turn left through a gate and follow the hedge to cross a stile and descend tricky steps to rejoin the main route opposite the track to **Yardworthy**.

The track leads to **Yardworthy Farm**, one of the oldest in the area. Pass the farmhouse (built in the 1700s), then bear right as signed into a field. Keep along the right edge of the next two fields. Cross a stile at the end and follow the narrow path half-left steeply downhill (slippery at times) into a wooded combe to cross the pretty South Teign river via a footbridge. Climb very steeply out of the valley, with increasingly good views to Meldon Hill to the right.

At the top follow a track alongside a boundary wall at Teignworthy. Pass through a gate between houses and along a track between high hedgebanks. By high gates bear left along a level path, following the wall.

The path ends at a gate; keep ahead between farm buildings to reach a lane at **Great Frenchbeer**. ▶ Cross the lane and go through a gate, then follow the fence below a wooden chalet. The lovely shaded

Meldon Hill towers over Chagford – seen here from the path near Teignworthy

The next section of the route, through a succession of small fields and patches of woodland to Teigncombe, is well signed.

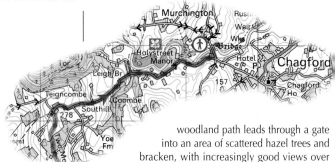

woodland path leads through a gate into an area of scattered hazel trees and bracken, with increasingly good views over the valley of the South Teign river to the right.

Follow the clearly signed path across stiles, through gates and fields and along sections of boardwalk over marshy ground, eventually crossing a small footbridge. Continue along the top edge of the next field, bearing left over a small stream at the end and through to gates to reach the lane at **Teigncombe**. ◄

The Mariner's Way keeps straight on towards Gidleigh.

Turn right down the track to reach a tarmac lane on a bend. Keep ahead; where the lane bears sharp right keep straight ahead on a narrower one that degenerates to a track at the gates to Northill and descends steeply to meet a lane to Gidleigh Park hotel.

Bear right, downhill, to cross **Leigh Bridge** over the South Teign, just above the confluence of North and South Teign rivers. This quiet lane passes listed **Holystreet Manor** – dating from the late 16th century, extensively rebuilt in the early 20th, and with a chapel dedicated to St Boniface – and later the kennels of the Mid Devon Hunt, to reach Factory Cross (note the ruined woollen mill on the left). At times there is a cupboard on the grass verge opposite offering snacks and drinks, with an honesty box for payment. ◄ Turn left to pass Corner Cottage and then cross the River Teign via medieval **Chagford Bridge**, to reach the end of Stage 5A.

Chagford lies under a mile to the right, up a steep hill.

STAGE 6

Chagford Bridge to Morchard Road

Start	Chagford Bridge (SX 694 880)
Finish	The A377 south of Morchard Road (SS 756 043)
Distance	18 miles (29km)
Time	8hrs
Terrain	River gorge, rolling farmland and wooded valleys
Maps	Explorer OL28 Dartmoor, 113 Okehampton; Landranger 191 Okehampton & North Dartmoor; Harvey Map Two Moors Way
Refreshments	Sandy Park Inn, Sandy Park (off route); Mill End Hotel, Dogmarsh Bridge; café at Castle Drogo (off route); Post Office Stores and The Drewe Arms, Drewsteignton; Ruby Red Farm Shop, Clannaborough Barton; Devonshire Dumpling pub, Morchard Road (off route)
Public toilets	None en route
Public transport	For Chagford: limited bus services to Okehampton, Exeter and Newton Abbot (via Moretonhampstead); for Morchard Road: Exeter to Barnstaple bus route and railway line (Tarka Line)
Parking	Laneside near Chagford Bridge (limited), pay & display in Chagford (off route); laneside off the A377 in Morchard Road
Accommodation	B&B, campsite, bunkhouse
Note	Stock up with food and drink at the village stores in Drewsteignton en route; there is no opportunity to buy anything until reaching the farm shop at Clannaborough Barton (closed on Sundays).

This stage initially follows the peaceful River Teign before passing Britain's 'youngest' castle, Castle Drogo, in a spectacular location overlooking the steep-sided Teign Gorge, to reach the pretty village of Drewsteignton. Thereafter the grand landscapes of Dartmoor are left behind as the Two Moors Way starts its 30-mile (48km) journey across the peaceful rolling farmland of Mid Devon. The route is generally well waymarked, and little walked: in high summer many of the paths tend to be overgrown but easily passable. After heavy rainfall expect deep and muddy stretches around field gates and on farm tracks.

This long stage can be most easily broken by diverting to Yeoford (a couple of miles off the route) after around 11¼ miles (18.25km).

Look out for kingfishers in summer. The upper Teign river is a popular fly-fishing venue (under licence) for salmon, sea trout and wild brown trout.

Once over the bridge, turn right through a gate on a signed footpath to pass a line of huge stone-girt oaks and through a gate to reach the river, passing a converted mill building on the opposite bank. ◄

The path runs through a succession of riverside meadows to reach a **weir**, at which point it leaves the river and follows a leat. Continue through fields to pass a footpath junction; keep ahead, signed to Rushford Bridge, to cross the leat on a footbridge. Bear half left to pass through the hedge, and continue in the same direction to meet the lane by double-arched 17th-century Rushford Bridge. Turn left, soon passing the swimming pool.

Chagford's rather special open-air **swimming pool**, near Rushford Mill, celebrated its 80th birthday in 2014. It was dug out by hand by local people on land given to the town by the Hayter Hames family, and the mill leat diverted to feed it. The water still comes from the leat, although these days it is filtered, and the beautifully maintained pool has undergone major refurbishments over the years.

A path soon passed to the left can be taken for a detour to the Sandy Park Inn, from where a field path leads back to the main route.

Turn right on a footpath into the yard at **Rushford Mill Farm**, keeping left of the farmhouse. The next gate leads into a level riverside meadow; pass an isolated granite gatepost to cut a river loop, then follow the riverbank into woodland. ◄

An interesting sculpture sits on a river island here: two halves of a granite 'ball'. This is *Granite Song* (1991), the work of internationally renowned sculptor and visual artist **Peter Randall-Page**, who lives at Veet Farm and whose installations also mark the start and end of the Mid Devon section of the Two Moors Way route.

Emerge from the woods to meet the A382 road by Dogmarsh Bridge. The **Mill End Hotel** – a 15th-century water-powered flourmill at its heart, and a hotel since 1929 – sits on the opposite bank of the river (open to non-residents).

The tranquil River Teign at Dogmarsh Bridge

Dartmoor was a popular tourist destination by the early 20th century, and in June 1911 the **Great Western Railway** started a through train service from Paddington to Moretonhampstead via Newton Abbot. From the end of the line at Moreton

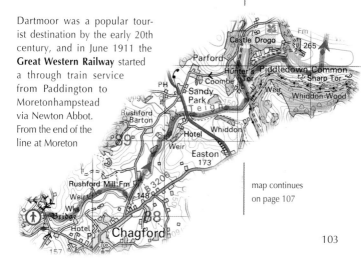

map continues on page 107

103

(a few miles to the south) visitors travelled by GWR motor omnibus to Chagford (and possibly to the Mill End Hotel). World War I put paid to the through service, and passenger services to Moretonhampstead stopped in 1959.

Cross the road with care, and enter the National Trust's **Castle Drogo** estate. The 'castle' can be seen ahead, perched on a bluff high above the valley. Follow the river through the level fields where the popular Chagford Show is held annually in the third week of August. A kissing gate leads into woodland at the entrance to the Teign Gorge and meets a path junction by an attractive suspension bridge. ◀

The Fisherman's Path follows the riverbank to Fingle Bridge and the Fingle Bridge Inn (around 2 miles/3.2km), from where the route can be rejoined via the Hunter's Path.

Turn left up a narrow woodland path. At the entrance to the thatched Gibhouse keep ahead up the drive. Just past a line of huge beeches turn sharp right to re-enter the Drogo estate, signed to Fingle Bridge, on the Hunter's Path, which soon swings sharp left along the top of the spectacular Teign Gorge. The earthworks of an Iron Age hillfort, Cranbrook Castle, are visible on the opposite side; Fingle Bridge is overlooked by another hillfort,

The Hunter's Path runs high above the Teign gorge

Prestonbury Castle, both fortifications dating from around 750BC. Occasional benches along the path tempt walkers to pause and drink in the amazing view! ▶

Castle Drogo is an impressive granite structure, designed by Sir Edwin Lutyens for the Home & Colonial Stores entrepreneur Sir Julius Drewe as a private home, and constructed between 1911 and 1930. Drewe chose this spot because of a fanciful notion that one 'Dru' or 'Drogo' – who was given the manor by William the Conqueror – was his ancestor. Sadly Drewe lost his beloved eldest son Adrian in World War I, a blow from which he never fully recovered. Over 60 percent of the castle's workforce was killed in action.

The path runs across the top of **Sharp Tor**; a fabulous viewpoint, but one to be treated with respect – recent clearance work has revealed just how precipitous the gorge is at this point.

At the next junction turn left up steps, as signed. Pass a bench and go through a kissing-gate into a big ridgetop field. Follow the left hedge to crest the ridge, enjoying good views over the little village of Drewsteignton and, on a clear day, Exmoor, more than 30 miles (48km) away. Descend steadily and into **Rectory Wood** via a gate. At a footpath junction take the very steep flight of steps in the direction of Drewsteignton, passing a small pumping station en route. At the next path junction keep straight on, ascending steeply to a lane.

Turn right, soon following the lane left into The Square at **Drewsteignton**, fringed by picturesque cob-and-thatch cottages. ▶

Drewsteignton's main claim to fame is that its pub, The Drewe Arms, once had the oldest licensee in the country: **Mabel Mudge**, who ran the establishment (initially with her husband Ernest) for 75 years until her retirement in 1994 at the age of 99. The pub – originally known as the Druid Arms,

Steps are soon passed leading up to the Castle Drogo visitor centre, café and toilets.

A small public garden above the lane on the left is a good picnic spot.

and comprised of several cottages – has changed since her time but retains its rustic and unspoiled atmosphere. Lovely Holy Trinity church, also on The Square, dates in part from the 16th century. Sir Julius Drewe, who instigated the pub's change of name, is buried in the churchyard at Drewsteignton under a Lutyens memorial.

Take the lane past the Post Office Stores, descending steeply past Netherton Cross to reach Veet Cross where the lane bears right. Keep ahead (unsigned) over a stream on a small bridge and head up the rough drive to **Veet Mill Farm**. Keep along a narrow path to the right of the property, then follow the stream gently uphill. The path levels and passes one half of Peter Randall-Page's Two Moors Way sculpture then ascends steeply to **Winscombe Farm**.

On meeting the drive turn left, still climbing, to reach the old A30. Cross over and turn left along the verge over the 'new' dual carriageway. A few paces later turn right down a farm drive at Brindlewood Farm. ◀ Cross a stile into a field and turn left down the hedge across rough ground, with good views towards the granite tower of Hittisleigh church. Cross the next high stile and continue downhill to cross another. Head towards

The next section of the route is well signed, although parts are overgrown in summer.

a thatched white farmhouse on the hill ahead, and over another a stile. Bear right, descending steeply to a stile into woodland. Cross the brook on a narrow plank to reach a footpath post; turn left under holly and hazel, amid bluebells in May.

map continues on page 109

Emerge onto a track, and cross the River Yeo on a footbridge. Ascend to a lane below West Ford Farm and turn right. About 50yds later (at the gate to Forder Cottage) bear left up steps into a field via a gate. Turn left to climb steeply alongside the fence, and keep in the same direction across the next field. The next stile leads to a rough field path that passes to the right of **Hill Farm**, wet underfoot in places. Bear right under lofty oaks; ignore an old footpath sign pointing right and head downhill to cross a stream in the bottom left corner of the next rough field. Ascend a fenced path and cross a boardwalk; keep along the right edge of the next field. At the end turn right to reach the drive to **Whitethorn Farm**. Follow the farm lane left, eventually ascending to the lane by thatched Grove Cottage.

Turn right past The Old Smithy and the former school and schoolhouse to reach Hittisleigh Cross. Keep straight on to find St Andrew's Church by beautiful **Hittisleigh Barton**.

The remote little hilltop settlement of **Hittisleigh** has a forgotten feel, and the parish once provided the poorest church income in Devon. The former working smithy and school building are testament to a time when the settlement had to be more self-sufficient than required today. The simple Church of St Andrew dates from the 1500s and is one of the loveliest in the area, with early 17th-century box pews. The views back to Cosdon Hill on the northeast corner of Dartmoor enhance a picnic break in the unspoiled churchyard.

107

Cosdon Hill on Dartmoor's northeastern edge can be seen from the churchyard at Hittisleigh

Follow the quiet ridgetop lane on for a further 2 miles (3.2km), keeping ahead at Howard Cross, Road Down Cross and Binneford Cross.

Alternative route to Road Down Cross

An alternative route (unsigned) can be followed from Howard Cross to Road Down Cross. It is intended to reduce the amount of lane walking on this stage: but since the alternative route involves at least a mile along the lane it seems of little benefit. Turn left at Howard Cross towards **Howard Barton**, soon picking up a path bearing right and dropping through fields and woodland to meet a lane. Turn right to pick up the main route again at Road Down Cross.

Keep straight on for a couple of miles to reach the village of Yeoford (pub and railway station).

Enjoy far-reaching views over field gates, especially looking north across Devon's heartland towards the southern slopes of Exmoor. About 500yds after Binneford Cross the way is signed left down a dead-end lane to Great Hele and **Newbury**. ◀ The lane descends steeply, bearing right to cross the **River Troney**. About 25yds later follow a bridlepath right and climb steeply up a deeply embanked track to enter sweeping fields. Keep along the left edge of two fields, and through a gate onto a track to reach a lane at a T-junction at **West Wotton**. Turn right downhill for 800yds to pass Granny's Meadow nursery.

About 25yds later (at **Prestons**) turn left down a track, which reduces to a path alongside Horwell Wood. ▸ Follow Two Moors Way roundels through a larch plantation to a crossing point on the single-track Exeter to Okehampton railway line, and continue through a rough plantation of larch, willow and silver birch.

For Colebrooke keep straight on along the lane.

This section of the former **London & South Western Railway**, from Coleford Junction to Okehampton, opened in 1871 (and was extended on to Lydford and Tavistock around the edge of Dartmoor in 1874). Take care crossing the line: although regular passenger services were withdrawn in 1972, and freight services only in 2011 with the closure of Meldon Quarry, the heritage trains of the Dartmoor Railway, based at Okehampton, still run at certain times of year.

Cross a brook on a footbridge and ascend a rough and wet hedged green lane (Webber's Lane); look out for badger setts in the rich red-earth banks. Emerge at a T-junction of lanes at Whelmstone Cross.

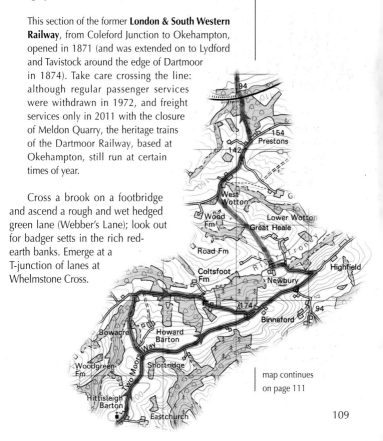

map continues on page 111

109

On this section of the Two Moors Way the **rich red soils** typical of this part of Mid Devon (and very much associated with the east of the county) become evident in the pastoral landscape. This characteristic colouring derives from iron oxides present in sandstones laid down in the arid desert conditions of the Permian and Triassic periods, 290 to 206 million years ago.

Keep straight on, downhill, to pass 15th-century cob-and-thatch farmhouse of **Whelmstone Barton**, first recorded in 1249. The lane ascends, with good views across the fields to the 14th/15th-century church of St Andrew at Colebrooke. Look for a footpath leading left across a red-earth field to a gate and footpath junction. ◄ Once through the gate bear left down a muddy track to another junction (with discretionary access to Ladywell Pond signed to the left). Cross the field ahead, aiming for the garden fence of a former coach house,

Here the Two Moors Way joins the route of the Devonshire Heartland Way as far as Appledore Farm.

The characteristic red soils of Mid Devon are clearly visible in fields at Whelmstone Cross

then follow the fence alongside the drive leading to **Paschoe House**, an imposing Tudor Gothic building dating from the mid 19th century.

At the end of the field the path leads left across the drive, and runs over a wide strip of gravel to the left of buildings at Paschoe Dairy Farm, including an impressive clock tower. Follow signs right then left along the field edge, then keep alongside the right edge of two fields, climbing steadily. At the top pass through a gate and turn right towards woodland, then pick up a track that zigzags downhill towards Georgian **Appledore Farm** (where the right of way has been diverted). On reaching farm buildings bear left, then right on a concrete way. Keep ahead through two gates, then cross the field (parallel to the farm drive) to reach a lane via a gate.

Pass through the gate opposite, and turn right up steps. Follow the hedge uphill towards white thatched buildings at **Sweetfield**. Cross a stile and stream, soon turning left alongside the garden hedge. At a footpath post turn right to cross a huge and sweeping field via an uncultivated strip. Pass through a gap in the hedge ahead and continue downhill on a track. At a path junction follow the track right, uphill, soon running along the top of another huge level field with fantastic views back to Dartmoor. Reach the farm drive at **Clannaborough Barton** opposite the pretty little church with its pinnacled tower, and turn left.

Clannaborough – a small parish with no village – was listed as a Domesday manor, although the present house dates from only around 1800. The interior of the simple 16th-century church was over-restored in the mid 1800s, and is dedicated to the Celtic St Petrock.

Keep to the verge and beware fast-moving traffic.

The very small village of Down St Mary with its medieval church lies along the lane to the left.

Take extreme care on the A377. For facilities at Morchard Road follow Stage 7 to Shobrooke Bridge, turning left to reach the A377 near the hub of the settlement.

The drive leads to the **A3072** between Copplestone and Bow. ◄ Turn right for 150yds, then cross over and follow the lane past **Lammacott Farm** to a junction. Turn right along a muddy track past farm buildings and a gate on the left. At the next gate (a Two Moors Way roundel on the right of the track is partially hidden) turn left down a frequently very muddy track, which bears right at the bottom of the field; turn left and follow the path through woodland, a field, and back into woodland. Cross a footbridge; turn right and head across a boggy field, then through another to reach the lane by **Barn Shelley**. ◄

Turn right. At the end of an oak avenue turn left over a stile and cross the field, aiming for a solitary oak and hedge corner. Follow the hedgebank, bearing left at the end to reach the busy A377 south of **Morchard Road**. Turn left along the verge, then cross the road at a Two Moors Way signpost. ◄

The rather unprepossessing settlement of **Morchard Road** is a staging post for travellers on the main A377 from Copplestone to Barnstaple, and the railway station, bus stop and pub are all accessed from Shobrooke Bridge. The arrival of the Exeter to Barnstaple turnpike road along the valley in the early 19th century – and the railway in mid-century – severely compromised the development of the area's ridgetop villages such as Down St Mary and Morchard Bishop, which were then relatively cut off until the use of cars became commonplace after World War II.

STAGE 7
Morchard Road to Witheridge

Start	The A377 south of Morchard Road (SS 756 043)
Finish	Witheridge, The Square (SS 803 145)
Distance	11 miles (17.75km)
Time	5½hrs
Terrain	Hilly farmland and wooded combes; trackless and pathless fields
Maps	Explorer 113 Okehampton, 127 South Molton & Chulmleigh (tiny stretch), 114 Exeter & the Exe Valley; Landranger 191 Okehampton & North Dartmoor, 181 Minehead & Brendon Hills; Harvey Map Two Moors Way
Refreshments	Devonshire Dumpling pub, Morchard Road (off route); Church Street Stores & Café and The London Inn, Morchard Bishop; The Black Dog Inn, Black Dog (off route); village stores and The Mitre Inn, Witheridge
Public toilets	Witheridge
Public transport	For Morchard Road: Exeter to Barnstaple bus route and railway line (Tarka Line); for Witheridge: Exeter to Barnstaple (via Tiverton and South Molton) bus route
Parking	Laneside off the A377 in Morchard Road; The Square (free) at Witheridge
Accommodation	B&B, campsite
Note	Summer walkers can take advantage of the uncultivated strips left along the edge of many arable fields on this stage, which enable easy passage, but there are no obvious paths across pasture fields.

The approximate halfway mark is reached on this stage at Morchard Bishop, a lovely ridgetop village with far-reaching views ahead to Exmoor and back towards Dartmoor from the churchyard (an excellent picnic spot). On this stage walkers become deeply immersed in the lush dairy and arable farming landscapes of Mid Devon, visiting isolated hamlets and passing ancient farmsteads and churches and encountering few, if any, people. At day's end arriving at the small rural town of Witheridge – at one time an important staging post on the Exeter to Barnstaple road – feels like taking a step back

A beautiful green lane ascends to Weeke

in time, particularly on a hot summer's afternoon when the whole place appears to be in deep slumber.

From the A377 pass through a gate into a damp meadow then bear left as signed, alongside the railway line.

> The '**Tarka Line**' (the old London & South Western Railway) opened in 1854 between Crediton and Barnstaple, mainly following the Taw valley (which is joined a few miles north of Morchard Road). Thankfully this delightful line survived Beeching's axe and has become known as the Tarka Line in honour of the North Devon novelist Henry Williamson, author of *Tarka the Otter*, whose work was so inspired by the 'Land of the Two Rivers'.

The path leads to Shobrooke Bridge; turn right on the track over the railway line. ▶ At the end of the first huge field (**Shobrooke Farm** ahead: private) turn left downhill and follow the field edge to reach a stile in an oak hedgebank. Stay alongside the left edge of the next field to reach a path junction.

For facilities at Morchard Road turn left here.

Turn left through a kissing gate and walk alongside woodland, and through a gate. Follow the right edge of the next field, gently uphill, towards a huge oak tree. At the field end turn right on a track towards buildings at **Slade**. The path bears left to pass the northern end of a line of pretty wildlife ponds, then leads through a gate into an orchard to meet a path junction. Turn right uphill through a gate to another junction.

Turn left along the edge of a deciduous plantation, with oak and cherry, pink purslane and cow parsley in early summer. Bear left through a gate and over a boardwalk, and along the left edge of the next field. A gate leads to a rocky green lane, which ascends, its banks carpeted with wildflowers in spring, to meet a tarmac lane by Middle Weeke Farm.

Turn right; after 50yds bear left at the gates to **Weeke Farm** along a track that descends to a junction. Keep ahead past **Woodgate House** and then a small cob barn with a corrugated-iron roof, Squirrel Lodge. Look carefully to spot the remnants of the original thatch under the 'modern' roof.

The beautiful narrow hedged path continues over a path crossroads, and through a gate into a field; aim for a hedge gap to the right of an oak tree. Continue in the same direction to pass two more oaks. Bear left at a footpath post to cross a stream, then ascend a short hedged track to meet four gates. Bear right through the second and ascend the right edge of a pasture field to reach houses on the edge of **Morchard Bishop**. Look back for wonderful views towards Dartmoor.

Cross a stile and follow a fenced path to the left of Higher Parks and through fields full of alpacas to meet a path junction by Linhay. Turn right to reach Fore Street; The London Inn is to the right.

Looking back towards Dartmoor from lush fields near Morchard Bishop

The rambling village of **Morchard Bishop** once stood on an important coach road – today's Fore Street – that ran between Barnstaple and Exeter, and thereafter continued on to London (which is the reason for the London Inn's name). Fore Street is also home to what is reputed to be the longest continuous row of thatched cottages in England, dating in the main from the late 18th century. The coming of the new road and railway in the valley, combined with a decline in the woollen industry (as wars with France closed European markets) resulted in a drop in population in the late 19th century. Today walkers can refresh themselves at the London Inn or at the Church Street Stores & Café, where takeaway drinks and food may also be purchased.

Cross over and down Church Street, soon passing the Stores & Café and later the Memorial Hall. ▶ The church of St Mary the Virgin dates from the 15th century and sits in a prominent position; its almost hundred foot high tower can be seen from miles around. From the church the lane drops towards an unexpectedly large car park; turn left along its upper edge. Note the Two Moors Way stone on the laneside. At a path junction keep ahead along the left field edge to reach another path junction; bear diagonally right across the field towards Morchard Wood, passing through a gate to reach another junction.

Morchard Bishop has an interesting early history, and Morchard Wood is a remnant of the **Great Wood** (the name Morechard comes from the Celtic words for great wood *mor* and *cet*), which is thought to have covered most of Devon before the seventh century. There is evidence of a Celtic site at Rudge, west of the village above the River Yeo, and a later Iron Age settlement to the southwest of the modern parish. The

St Gatien Garden on Church Street – the village is twinned with the village of St Gatien des Bois in Normandy – is an ideal picnic spot.

map continues on page 119

117

manor became the property of the Bishop of Exeter in the 1207, which is the reason for the suffix added to the village's name.

Resist any temptation to bear left into the wood here, and instead keep ahead alongside a metal fence. At its end bear left to find a kissing gate into the east end of the wood. Bear half-right on a track and descend to reach a quiet lane.

Turn left towards **Beech Hill Cross**. After 50yds turn right through two gates and follow a broad track along the bottom edge of a fields, soon alongside a post-and-wire fence parallel to Belkay Copse, eventually dropping steeply to pass through a gate under a lovely oak tree and cross the infant River Creedy. Ascend through woodland (bluebells in May) and through a gate into the next field; climb steeply up the left edge, towards buildings at **Lower Brownstone Farm**. In the top corner bear left through a metal gate. Skirt dilapidated barns, guided by a footpath post. At the next post turn right; a gate leads down steps to a farm lane. Turn left to reach a lane.

Cross over and pass Orchard End Kennels on a woodland track. Go through the left of two gates at the end and continue along the right edge of a two initially damp fields (look out for cuckoo flower in summer). At the end cross a stile and turn right through a gate; descend diagonally left across the next beautiful pasture field, towards woodland. Cross a stream and go through a gate; climb steeply up the right edge of the next three fields, towards a large barn at the top. A deeply rutted track runs along the right edge of the next field to reach a lane.

Cross over, passing through a gate into a field: Cobscombe Farm, seen on the hill ahead, is the next port of call. Follow signs diagonally right and through a gate, then bear right along boardwalks and over two stiles. Walk straight up the next field and through a gate; follow the track ahead past chicken houses and the farmhouse to reach the lane at Lower Black Dog. Turn right; soon note a small cob building on the right.

In Devon's heartland – and over much of Southwest England – **cob** was the traditional wall-building material used up to the mid 19th century: a mix of readily available straw, sand, earth and water. A revival of interest in sustainable building techniques has led to a new (if small) wave of cob construction for domestic homes. An old Devon saying states that cob needs 'a good hat and a good pair of boots': unless cob walls are protected by (originally) thatch, and latterly (usually) corrugated iron, they quickly become waterlogged and deteriorate.

About 75yds beyond The Old Post Office turn sharp left down a pleasant track towards **Pyne Farm** (Two Moors Way sign concealed by the hedge). ▶ Descend to cross a stream; ascend past the scheduled cob-and-thatch farmhouse with its cob-walled garden and through a gate into a field. Follow the hedge, soon dropping steeply to cross a stile at the bottom. Cross a footbridge then ascend steeply along the right edge of two fields, passing to the right of buildings at **Wonham Farm** and through a gate. Cross the farm drive and pass through a big gate.

Walk downhill along the right edge of the next field; where the hedge ends bear right over a stile. Keep straight on as signed, soon crossing a stile, along the hedgebank and then a wire fence, soon dropping downhill into Washford Wood via a footbridge. The path climbs

For The Black Dog Inn keep ahead for 200yds.

map continues on page 120

steeply before levelling. Lovely oaks and beech rise out of a carpet of bluebells in late spring, evidence of old and undisturbed woodland.

At the end of the wood a hedged path meets a lane on a corner. Turn left to reach the little hamlet of **Washford Pyne**.

Washford Pyne was recorded in the Domesday Book as Waseforde, which may mean 'the ford by the rapids'. **St Peter's Church**, seemingly in the middle of nowhere, dates only from the late 19th century, after it was rebuilt following a disastrous fire in around 1880. It is thought that parts of the original church dated from the 13th century. On a hot day walkers will be pleased to find a supply of bottled water and cups in this neat little church, the tower of which – unusually – is topped with a small wooden spire. A glance at the visitors' book reveals the signatures of many Two Moors Way/Coast to Coast walkers.

Immediately before the church turn left down a track past the Georgian rectory, descending into woodland. Bear left as signed on a sunken track, then cross a stile into a narrow meadow, damp underfoot. Cross a broad stream – the River Dalch – on a substantial footbridge and keep ahead up the next rough pasture field, aiming to the right of a solitary beech tree. Pass through a small gate and keep along the left edge of the next field. At a footpath post bear left and follow the track past the ornamental gates to **Stourton Barton** to meet a concrete track by farm buildings. Turn right to follow the drive downhill past ponds and up to a lane.

Cross over and go through a gate; cross two fields towards Millmoor Farm, aiming to the left of the farmhouse. A gate leads onto the farm drive; turn left to meet the road. Cross over and down the drive to **Woodford Farm**. Before reaching buildings bear right through a

Washford Pyne's Church of St Peter: perfectly placed for a short break

gate and follow a track up the left edge of fields to the hilltop, with views of Witheridge church ahead. ▶ Turn right through a gate and descend the left edge of a field; about 200yds before the end turn right across an uncultivated strip to cross a footbridge by a big oak tree. Head up the middle of the next field, and the next, to find a footpath junction. Keep straight on to reach the end of a cul-de-sac (Wiriga Way – *wiriga* being the name for the settlement as recorded in the Domesday Book, and interpreted as 'ridge with withies', or 'wethers'). Follow the road past bungalows to find a narrow high-fenced path between the gardens of mid-19th-century village houses to emerge by the Post Office and Stores and reach The Square in **Witheridge**.

There are excellent views north to Exmoor and south to Dartmoor on a clear day.

Witheridge – like Morchard Bishop and so many of Mid Devon's ridgetop settlements – has been bypassed, but this time within the modern era: the North Devon link road from Tiverton to Barnstaple,

Witheridge has its share of picturesque thatched cottages

built in the late 1980s, has drawn traffic and business away from this long-established agricultural settlement (11 of the parish's farms are recorded in the Domesday book). The heart of the town in a conservation area and the huge square – dating from Saxon times – was once the venue for fairs and markets, and until relatively recently was overlooked by four inns. Today Witheridge has one pub, The Mitre (accommodation and takeaway meals), built as a coaching inn in the 1830s. The substantial church of St John the Baptist still has a late 13th-century chancel, but the bulk of the building dates from the 15th century, with extensive internal Victorian restoration when the gallery and box pews were removed.

STAGE 8

Witheridge to Knowstone

Start	Witheridge, The Square (SS 803 145)
Finish	Knowstone, church steps (SS 828 231)
Distance	8¼ miles (13.25km)
Time	4hrs
Terrain	Field paths and woodland tracks, commons, quiet country lanes
Maps	Explorer 114 Exeter & the Exe Valley; Landranger 181 Minehead & Brendon Hills; Harvey Map Two Moors Way
Refreshments	The Mitre Inn, Witheridge; Log Cabin Diner at the A361 rest area, Knowstone Moor; The Masons Arms, Knowstone
Public toilets	Witheridge; rest area on the A361, Knowstone Moor
Public transport	For Witheridge: Exeter to Barnstaple (via Tiverton and South Molton) bus route; no public transport to Knowstone
Parking	The Square (free) at Witheridge; by the church in Knowstone
Accommodation	B&B
Note	Stock up with food and drink at the village stores in Witheridge; there is no opportunity to buy anything until the A361 is reached (and no obvious picnic places until the Link Road rest area, where most walkers prefer not to linger other than to buy an ice cream or drink on a hot day).

The majority of this stage is even quieter than Stage 7. No villages, hamlets or shops are passed (until the refreshment area just off the A361), and it is unlikely that you will see much in the way of wheeled traffic, despite a three-mile (4.8km) stretch of quiet country lane north of Bradford Moor. You will, however, come across plenty of wildlife and wildflowers in spring and summer. The North Devon link road comes as something of a shock as cars and lorries hurtle through the ancient commonland of Knowstone Outer and Inner Moors, but this is quickly left behind on the narrow lane that drops towards the secluded hamlet of Knowstone.

map continues
on page 127

Cross the road from the bus stop on the B3137 at the The Square in **Witheridge** and turn right to pass The Mitre Inn. Take the first lane left, signed to Rackenford. Just past the village hall and playground turn left through a kissing gate. The next gate leads to a field; descend alongside the left edge, the follow a narrow hedged path into a field. Bear half-right towards the hedge (if planted with crops a path is usually left for walkers) and then follow that downhill into the Woodland Trust's Yeo Copse.

The deeply banked path descends to a path junction; follow the main path right to exit the woodland and meet a brook, a tributary of the **Little Dart River**. Keep along the right bank through buttercup water meadows, then cross over via a footbridge and pass through a gate. Pass a Two Moors Way sign to walk along the lower edge of a huge pasture field, left of a line of big oak trees. Continue in the same direction in the next field. Where the Little Dart loops away keep ahead to pass to the left of a big ash tree, aiming for a hedge corner. Cross a stream via a big footbridge and boardwalks over boggy ground. Cross the next meadow, then skirt a coniferous plantation.

Wildlife is plentiful in this undisturbed and little-walked part of Mid Devon, and you may be lucky enough to see a hare in these riverside meadows. The woodlands provide cover for fallow deer, and buzzards can frequently be spotted soaring high in the sky above.

The path bears away from the trees to pass through a gate to reach an enormous level field. Keep along the right edge, passing through two gates to meet the lane by Bradford Moor House.

This damp clayey field is **Bradford Moor**: unimproved pasture rich in old-fashioned species, thick with early purple and marsh orchids, sorrel, ox-eye daisies, buttercups and ragged robin in early summer, and alive with butterflies.

Turn left, past summer hedgerows bursting with dog rose, foxglove, bird's-foot trefoil and red campion. Cross Bradford Bridge over the Little Dart by **Bradford Mill**, a working mill from the 17th to 20th centuries. Climb steeply to reach a fork at Bradford Cross, and keep left

Bradford Moor

Ducks in the orchard at Bradford Barton

At the brow of the hill, about 400yds later, look south for views as far as Haytor on Dartmoor's southern edge.

The lane across Knowstone Moor is unfenced and walkers may choose to walk across open ground if they wish.

(signed Creacombe and Rose Ash) to pass **Bradford Barton**. Keep ahead at Crowdhole Cross, and turn right to Rackenford at **Parsonage Cross**. Pass straight over Creacombe Moor Cross, climbing to over 800ft (247m) above sea level and enjoying sweeping views over rolling farmland from this high vantage point, and towards the southern slopes of Exmoor. ◄ The lane levels off to reach the Old Toll House (on what was the main turnpike from Tiverton to South Molton in the 18th century) on the B3221 at Backstone Cross.

Bear left and cross the road to pick up a green lane, muddy in places, between beech hedgebanks. Cross a high hedgebank via a ladderstile and walk on to emerge onto the edge of **Knowstone Outer Moor**. Bear left at a Two Moors Way sign along the edge on the common to reach a lane. Turn left, downhill. ◄

On the OS map the two Knowstone Moors and nearby Hares Down (SSSI) form an island of open access land surrounded by a tightly packed network of small fields. These three areas together form Devon's largest remaining block of now rare **culm grassland** (purple moor-grass pasture and wet heath) – which once covered much of the north of the county. It's hard not to be distracted by the link road traffic, but look out for heath spotted orchids, ragged robin and marsh fritillary butterflies. Locals with common grazing rights have kept cattle here for centuries. This type of grassland has an extraordinary ability to absorb water: five times the rate of ordinary grassland.

The lane crosses a stream at the bottom of the hill. ▶ Turn right along a series of boardwalks over boggy ground to pass under the A361: thankfully the path has been built – admittedly across somewhat unsuitable ground – to avoid walkers having to cross the busy road. The path threads its way through a strip of light woodland on the edge of **Knowstone Inner Moor** to reach a lane; turn left.

For the Log Cabin Diner and toilets keep straight on.

At the next lane junction turn right towards **Knowstone**. On the left here a surprisingly unsympathetic block of worked granite celebrates the Millennium in Knowstone parish. Follow the lane downhill, looking for a stile on the right at a Two Moors Way sign. Descend along the left edge of two fields; turn left over a stile and head towards the church to find a fenced path that leads to the churchyard. Turn left to reach the lane opposite the 13th-century thatched Masons Arms.

127

The Masons Arms is in the heart of Knowstone

Knowstone is a pretty little hamlet – and a designated conservation area – which, despite its proximity to the busy road, feels remarkably remote. The 15th-century church of St Peter is mainly medieval and has a 12th-century doorway; the wonderfully unspoiled churchyard is awash with ox-eye daisies in summer. Great Wadham, a farm to the northwest of the hamlet, has a connection with Oxford University: the widow of Sir Nicholas Wadham was born here, and his widow founded Wadham College in his memory. Local facilities for walkers are very limited; The Masons Arms has a Michelin-starred restaurant but no accommodation.

STAGE 9
Knowstone to Tarr Steps

Start	Knowstone, church steps (SS 828 231)
Finish	Tarr Steps (SS 868 361)
Alternative Finish	Withypool, General Stores (SS 846 335)
Distance	10 miles (16km); or 12¼ miles (19.7km)
Time	4½hrs; or 5¼hrs
Terrain	Rolling fields and wooded valleys
Maps	Explorer 114 Exeter & the Exe Valley, OL9 Exmoor; Landranger 181 Minehead & Brendon Hills; Harvey Map Two Moors Way
Refreshments	The Masons Arms, Knowstone; Tarr Farm Inn, Tarr Steps; ice cream kiosk at Tarr Steps (seasonal); The Royal Oak Inn and General Stores, Withypool (alternative finish)
Public toilets	None en route; Tarr Steps (off route)
Public transport	None
Parking	By the church in Knowstone; car park at Tarr Steps (charge); car park by Withypool Bridge (free, alternative finish)
Accommodation	B&B
Note	On this stage forward planning with regard to food and drink en route is essential: no shops or refreshment stops are passed until the Barle is crossed at Tarr Steps, or Withypool reached (alternative finish).

All thoughts of the cars and lorries racing along the intrusive A361 North Devon link road are rapidly left behind on this tranquil stage, which explores the hills and combes typical of Exmoor's southern hinterland. The route leaves the pretty village of Knowstone and visits the lovely church at West Anstey before a long uphill stretch gains the edge of West Anstey Common and the start of Exmoor 'proper'. The day ends at one of Exmoor's tourist hotspots, the impressive clapper bridge spanning the River Barle just north of Hawkridge. Devastating floods (in late 2012 and during autumn 2013) damaged the clapper bridge at Tarr Steps to such an extent that it was temporarily rendered impassable. To accommodate such an (unusual) event, there is an alternative finish at Withypool.

Unrestored round house at Owlaborough

From the church steps turn right to pass The Masons Arms. At Greenhill Cross turn left down a dead end lane to cross a footbridge over the evocatively named Crooked Oak stream. The lane climbs uphill past **Owlaborough**.

map continues
on page 132

The interesting stone-built structure with a corrugated-iron roof seen at Owlaborough is an old **roundhouse**, often these days restored as a stylish extension to a converted barn. These usually once held the wherewithal for threshing the grain from the chaff by the use of horse power, the horse being harnessed to a central beam and walking around the inside edge of the building, thus driving the machinery within. The example here was used as a cider press.

130

The track deteriorates past Highfield Farm; at a fork keep left. Where the track bears away right pass through the gate ahead, along a green lane, and through a gate into a field. Reach a barn on the edge of sweeping pasture fields on Owlaborough Moor, then follow the right field edge past a line of beech trees, to find a gate in the wire fence. Clip the bottom corner of the next field, aiming for a gate by a twisted beech tree. Cross the next field in the same direction to find a stile by a gate in the top right corner by New Moor Plantation. Turn left to reach the B3227, the old main road from South Molton to Taunton via Bampton but now very quiet. The expanse of West Anstey Common – and the onward route – comes into tempting and sharp focus here.

Turn right for 100yds, then left over a stile. ▶ Keep along the right edge of two fields, towards Higher Barton Farm. About 100 metres before reaching a barn bear left across the field and through a gate. Follow the right field edge past the back of barns and over a stile (sometimes impeded by old farm machinery) onto the lane.

The permitted path from here to the lane near Highaton Head Cross is passable, but at times is not easy for walkers.

The route passes a wind-sculpted beech on Owlaborough Moor

Turn right to reach Highaton Head Cross, and turn left downhill towards Yeo Mill, soon passing between the piers of a dismantled railway line.

This was the 43-mile (69km) single-track **Devon & Somerset Railway**, a branch line from Norton Fitzwarren near Taunton to Barnstaple, opened in 1873 and operated by the Bristol & Exeter Railway Company. The line closed in 1966.

map continues on page 135

Continue through the tiny village of **Yeo Mill**. Partridge Arms Farm – a former coaching inn – and The Old Shop (now a cottage) both bear witness to a time when such villages were more self-sufficient. Cross the **River Yeo** and pass Mill House to reach a staggered cross-roads at Yeo Mill Cross.

Turn right along a narrow and unsigned lane, dropping to cross the West Anstey stream. Ascend past Higher Wychwood, where homemade produce is sometimes on sale at the laneside. As the lane starts to drop turn left up a steeply ascending green lane, then continue up the left edge of a field and past the Elizabethan Plantation, a copse of hazel trees planted in 1992 to mark the 40th anniversary of the accession of Queen Elizabeth II. Stay along the left hedge, soon dropping onto a sunken path and through a gate onto the lane opposite the beautiful Old Vicarage in **West Anstey**, and turn right.

Take a quick detour up the 'No Through Road' to tranquil **St Petrock's Church** (a good place to take a break), which dates from the 14th century. The tower was added in the mid 1400s, and the church – having fallen into disrepair – underwent major restoration in the late 19th century. A vast number of Devon's churches have suffered Victorian 'improvement', but St Mary's at Molland, a mile or

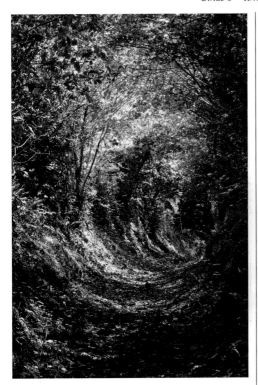

An atmospheric old green lane leads towards West Anstey

two to the west, is the most perfect example of an unspoilt Georgian church found in the county, with high box pews, flagstone floors, a canopied three-decker pulpit and ornate 17th- and 18th-century monuments. Make a mental note to visit this wonderful building another day.

The lane ascends, giving lovely views back over the church and Church House. Follow the lane past the entrance to **Badlake Farm** and climb very steeply for over a mile to reach Badlake Moor Cross on the edge of Woodland Common.

133

A rather lovely bench provides a comfortable resting place for a breather; pause for a moment to enjoy a last look back to Dartmoor.

Turn left through the gate by the cattle grid, then cross the lane to reach the 'official' start of the Exmoor section of the Two Moors Way and Peter Randall-Page's sculpture tucked under the beech hedgebank. Follow the rough path alongside the bank to reach the next lane on the edge of **West Anstey Common**. ◄ Cross the lane and follow the track, soon starting to descend with lovely views towards Hawkridge, perched 1000ft (305m) above sea level on a prominent ridge between the River Barle and its tributary, the Dane's Brook.

Two **Bronze Age barrows** (gorse-covered mounds today) sit on the common to the left of the track, both excavated in the early 19th century. Whereas Exmoor's Bronze Age legacy is far less prolific than Dartmoor's, barrows, standing stones and stone rows can be seen – the latter mainly of a type found in South Wales, and mostly found in this, the western end of the national park.

Pass through thickets of gorse and, as the track widens, look carefully for a signpost to the left (permitted path to Slade Bridge). This initially indistinct and damp path, at times boggy and at others stony, drops steadily towards the lowest point of the Dane's Brook valley, roughly in line with a lane seen climbing steeply up the other side.

At this point the walker crosses from Devon into Somerset; the boundary follows the brook for a short distance.

Look left for lovely views up the valley and to spot the Venford Stone, thought to be a 19th-century boundary stone for land belonging to Venford Farm, under a mile to the southeast. Drop through scattered silver birch and mountain ash to reach the lane and turn left downhill to cross **Dane's Brook** at Slade Bridge. ◄

Slade Lane ascends steeply; where it bends left keep ahead through a gate and continue to climb steeply across a big pasture field, aiming for the top left corner, and onto the lane again by West Hollowcombe Farm. Turn right to reach a lane junction in the centre of **Hawkridge**, where a rustic seat circles a solitary copper beech tree by the old village pump.

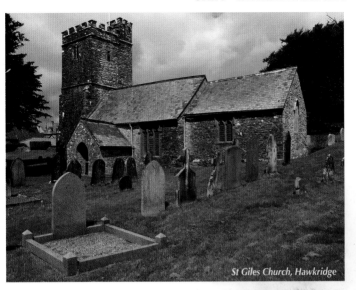

St Giles Church, Hawkridge

Hawkridge is one of Exmoor's most remote and least visited villages. Arthur Mee in his wonderful *The King's England* volume on the county states that in the 1940s there were no telephones or telephone wires here; cars were rarely seen, and no one in the village had one; and it comes as no surprise to learn that the village was cut off for 10 days as a result of heavy snowfall in the winter of 1978. Take time to visit the simple little church of St Giles, mainly dating from the 14th and 15th centuries. Peer through the window of Tom Lock's workshop in the village 'centre'; the Lock family started making gates and carts here in 1840. Tom was born in Hawkridge and has crafted unique articles for years, using shed red deer antlers.

Turn left along the lane signed to Withypool. After 150yds bear right across grass and up steps to pass through a gate,

map continues on page 136

The Two Moors Way follows the River Barle or its valley from this point all the way to Simonsbath.

soon crossing a stile. Bear left across the field, aiming for a gate by a big beech tree. Bear half right in the next field, towards a gap in the beech hedgebank, with increasingly good views over the wooded valley of the River Barle. ◄ Keep along the bottom of next field, dropping to a stile in the corner above Great Cleave.

The sunken path ahead follows the right hedgebank initially and is very muddy at first, but soon improves. Keep straight ahead and through a gate in the next hegebank, soon descending gently to find a gate onto a lane above Rowdown Wood. Follow the lane ahead to pick up a footpath to **Parsonage Farm**. Descend to cross a stream, then follow the track uphill, passing to the left of the farmhouse and through gates to reach a field. After a few paces meet a path junction (SS 858 320).

Alternative finish at Withypool

To bypass Tarr Steps, turn left on the bridleway (signed to Withypool Hill) and follow the beech hedgebank, ascending gently. Keep in the same direction in the next field; the swell of Withypool Hill comes into view ahead.

Pass through the next gate and along the edge of the next field, then through a gate onto a raised bank – usually muddy – with good views towards **Westwater Farm** and Withypool Hill. Descend through a metal gate, then cross the field to reach the lane by the farm. Turn right to climb steeply over **Withypool Hill** – the common is home to a herd of Exmoor ponies – before dropping into the small village of **Withypool**.

In medieval times **Withypool** – the name taken from the willows (withies) growing by the Barle – was the 'headquarters' of the Royal Forest. The twice-yearly Forest Court (Swainmote) was held a mile or so upstream at Landacre Bridge until James Boevey (see Stage 10) moved it to Simonsbath. St Andrew's Church – heavily restored in the late 19th century – was originally a chapel-of-ease for Hawkridge, servicing those living at some distance from the main parish church. RD Blackmore stayed at The Royal Oak in 1866 while writing *Lorna Doone*; the shooting of his heroine on her wedding day is said to have been inspired by the tale of Chagford's Mary Whiddon (see Stage 5).

Walkers can buy refreshments at the well-stocked village shop, which is also a local information point for Exmoor National Park.

If Tarr Steps is impassable, Withypool Bridge has to be crossed to rejoin the main route

Cross the **River Barle** via six-arched Withypool Bridge – which dates back over 100 years, and replaced a medieval packhorse bridge – and pass the toilets and café opposite the General Stores.

For the main route from the path junction at SS 858 320, keep straight on along the right edge of the next two fields. Drop to pass through a gate and descend very steeply, turning right down a sunken track at the end of the field; curve left into oak and beech woodland and follow the narrow and rocky path downhill to **Tarr Steps** and cross the River Barle – the name is said to derive from the Anglo Saxon *Beorgwella*, 'hill stream' – to reach a footpath junction below **Tarr Farm Inn**. ◀

The car park and public toilets can be found a short walk up the lane from the bridge.

Tarr Steps clapper bridge, situated at an ancient fording point of the Rive Barle, is probably Exmoor's most iconic site. Its time of original construction is unconfirmed, but many believe it dates from medieval times. It is the longest example in the country, with 17 spans; the stones are now all recorded so that they can be repositioned relatively easily should a section be washed away (in the floods of 1952 when Lynmouth suffered so terribly – see Stage 11 – all but two of the spans were washed away). Legend has it that the bridge was built by the Devil and that no one can cross when he chooses to lie on it to sunbathe!

STAGE 10

Tarr Steps to Simonsbath

Start	Tarr Steps (SS 868 321)
Alternative Start	Withypool, General Stores (SS 846 335)
Finish	Simonsbath, Ashcombe car park (SS 774 394)
Distance	11 miles (17.75km); or 6½ miles (10.5km)
Time	6hrs; or 3hrs
Terrain	Riverside paths, uneven and wet in places; open common
Maps	Explorer OL9 Exmoor; Landranger 181 Minehead & Brendon Hills, 180 Barnstaple & Ilfracombe; Harvey Map Two Moors Way
Refreshments	Tarr Farm Inn and ice cream kiosk (seasonal) at Tarr Steps; The Royal Oak Inn, Withypool and Withypool General Stores and Tearoom (tearoom seasonal); Boeveys Tea Rooms, Simonsbath House Hotel and Exmoor Forest Inn, Simonsbath
Public toilets	Tarr Steps (in car park); Withypool; Simonsbath
Public transport	None
Parking	Car park at Tarr Steps (off route, charge); Ashcombe car park, Simonsbath (donation)
Accommodation	B&B
Note	At times of exceptionally high water it may be necessary to divert from the main route (see 'Alternative route').

This stage follows the lovely River Barle pretty much all the way to the 'manufactured' 19th-century settlement at Simonsbath in the heart of the former Royal Forest of Exmoor. Although the gradients are generally gentle, underfoot conditions are less so, in that the popular riverside path from Tarr Steps to the historic village of Withypool is usually wet and muddy in patches and flood damage has rendered it uneven and battered in parts. The walk alongside the Barle towards Simonsbath, however, is one of the loveliest sections of the entire route and particularly so in summer when it is awash with wildflowers, butterflies, dragonflies and damselflies. As an added bonus Exmoor ponies may well be encountered on the common above historic Landacre Bridge, a little upriver from Withypool.

On rare occasions of very high water the path alongside the Barle may be impassable, in which case an alternative 6½-mile (10.5km) route can be followed to regain Simonsbath via Blue Gate.

The Barle is privately owned, and access to the water is only allowed at fords.

At the signpost below the **Tarr Farm Inn** turn left on a permitted path alongside the river. ◀ The path enters Knaplock Wood and joins a bridlepath, soon descending to a stone-built section alongside the water.

Much of the area around Tarr Steps is designated a Site of Special Scientific Interest. The steep valley sides support native **sessile oak** – the acorns have no stalks – along with ash, hazel and beech. In times past coppicing was carried out here: trees were cut periodically for fuel, charcoal, tanbark and building materials, then allowed to regrow.

The path climbs away from the river as the lane to Withypool is approached

At the end of the wood cross a footbridge and continue across a riverside meadow. This sets the pattern

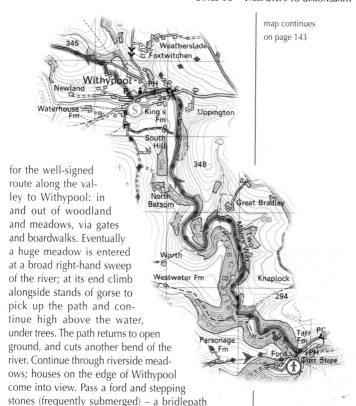

map continues
on page 143

for the well-signed route along the valley to Withypool: in and out of woodland and meadows, via gates and boardwalks. Eventually a huge meadow is entered at a broad right-hand sweep of the river; at its end climb alongside stands of gorse to pick up the path and continue high above the water, under trees. The path returns to open ground, and cuts another bend of the river. Continue through riverside meadows; houses on the edge of Withypool come into view. Pass a ford and stepping stones (frequently submerged) – a bridlepath via South Hill onto Withypool Common – then pick up a recently restored path that climbs across the heads of two small combes to reach the lane into **Withypool**.

Turn left downhill into the village, passing The Royal Oak Inn and St Andrews Church with its squat crenellated tower. ▶

About 100yds past the church – as the lane drops towards the village shop (toilets opposite) bear half-right on a dead-end lane. (The grassy bank on the southern side of the river, just over the bridge, is a lovely picnic spot.) After 100yds turn right by 'Moor View' signed to

If you finished Stage 9 at Withypool rejoin the main route at the lane junction just above the village shop.

141

Looking downstream towards historic Landacre Bridge

Kitridge Lane, soon passing the old Withypool Board School via a fenced path. Head across the next two fields; walk cross the third (narrowing) field to cross a stile in the far corner, onto a lane.

Turn left, ascending gently, to pass Kitridge Farm. About a mile later pass through a gate on a byway across open common, soon crossing Landacre Lane. At the next track junction (Thornmead is signed right) keep ahead, signed Simonsbath/Pickedstones. About 100yds later, where the track forks, keep right to skirt the head of a small combe and boggy ground; at the next signed junction keep ahead (Simonsbath via Cow Castle). ◀ The path soon bears left and starts to descend gently towards the Barle opposite the tributary valley of the **Sherdon Water**; look left for views of Landacre Bridge, and keep an eye out for Exmoor ponies.

The Simonsbath via Pickedstones path offers another option, but is not the official route.

Pass through a gate in a high hedgebank (built by the Knight family in 1824, and thus entering the former Royal Forest) and follow the path downhill, soon rounding the hillside through bracken-covered slopes and heading

down into a coniferous plantation via a gate alongside a line of lovely beech trees. Where the track turns left to a ford follow the bridleway ahead to pass a big footbridge over the **River Barle**.

Alternative route to Simonsbath via Blue Gate

If the river is exceptionally high the path alongside the Barle may be impassable, in which case cross the footbridge over the Barle and follow a beaten path across damp rushy

map continues
on page 145

The path drops towards the river (and the start of the alternative route to Simonsbath via Blue Gate)

ground to cross a stream and reach a track leading to a ford across the river. Turn right and climb steadily uphill for about a mile to reach the tarmac lane leading to **Horsen Farm**. Turn left along the lane for over 2 miles (3.2km) to the T-junction at **Blue Gate**, on the Simonsbath–Brayford road. The lofty Chains and Exe Plain come into clear view away to the right, as does steep-sided Tangs Bottom. Turn right and follow the lane, downhill, for 1½ miles (2.4km) to cross the River Barle via Simonsbath Bridge and reach the B3223. Turn right with care (no pavement) to pass the Exmoor Forest Inn and phone box to reach the entrance to Ashcombe car park on the left.

Stay alongside the River Barle (signed Simonsbath) for around 50yds to cross a footbridge over the tributary stream of White Water and pass through a gate. The bridlepath (initially wet underfoot) passes an outcrop known as The Calf and then bears right around the lower slopes of the hilltop Iron Age fort of **Cow Castle** – 'cow' deriving from the Celtic *caer* (fort). ◄ Follow an old slate wall back to the river and follow the lovely riverside path, passing through occasional gates. At a line of beautiful beech trees bear right to cut a bend of the river. Eventually pass the remains of buildings and workings at Wheal Eliza.

It may be tempting to skirt the left slope across Open Access land, but this is not the official route.

Cow Castle Iron Age fort is located at an old crossing point of the Barle

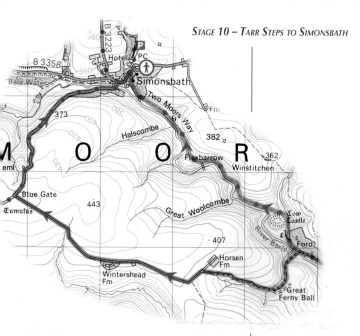

Wheal Eliza was a copper mine initiated by the Knight family, who were responsible for the development of Simonsbath during the 19th century. Cornish miners were employed, which is why the word *wheal*, the Cornish word for 'mine', is in the title. Although many of the Knights' schemes failed (including the mine, which only operated from 1846 to 1857), their various works transformed the local landscape.

The path bears away from the river to round the conical hill of **Flexbarrow**; Birchcleave Wood, planted by the Knights in the mid 19th century (said to be the highest beech wood in the country) comes into view ahead, the path running along its lower edge. ▶ Keep straight on at a path junction – towards the car park – to meet the road opposite the Exmoor Forest Inn in **Simonsbath**. Cross over and turn right past the phone box to reach the entrance to Ashcombe car park.

It is possible to divert here and walk through the riverside meadows (Open Access) if wished, towards Simonsbath Bridge.

145

In the Barle valley heading towards Simonsbath; Birchcleave Wood on the distant slopes

Simonsbath lies in the heart of the Royal Forest of Exmoor – not a forest in the established sense of the word, but a hunting ground for the king – which was confirmed in the 13th century. No buildings were permitted within the Forest boundary, but by the mid 17th century James Boevey, Warden of the Forest, had built a house at Simonsbath (the original part of the Simonsbath House Hotel: the date 1654 can be seen above a fireplace in the oldest part of the building). In 1818 a wealthy Midlands industrialist, John Knight, bought about 10,000 acres (4050ha) of the Royal Forest (later extending his estate even further) and set about various improvements: he and his son Frederic built St Luke's Church, a school (closed in 1970), sawmill, houses for those working in the copper and iron mines in the Barle valley, several farms and roads, and planted many of Exmoor's iconic beech hedgebanks. Walkers have a choice of venues for refreshment: pub, historic hotel or tea rooms, the last fittingly named after one of the Forest Wardens.

STAGE 11
Simonsbath to Lynmouth

Start	Simonsbath, Ashcombe car park (SS 774 394)
Finish	Lynmouth, The Pavilion on The Esplanade (SS 723 497)
Distance	11¼ miles (18km)
Time	6hrs
Terrain	Open common, rough paths and tracks, wooded valleys
Maps	Explorer OL9 Exmoor; Landranger 180 Barnstaple & Ilfracombe
Refreshments	Boeveys Tea Rooms, Simonsbath House Hotel and Exmoor Forest Inn, Simonsbath; Watersmeet Tearoom (off route); cafés and pubs in Lynmouth
Public toilets	Simonsbath; Watersmeet (off route); Lynmouth
Public transport	For Lynmouth: Lynmouth to Minehead and Barnstaple bus service (see Introduction)
Parking	Ashcombe car park, Simonsbath (donation); car parks at Lynmouth (pay & display)
Accommodation	B&B, campsite
Note	When crossing Dure Down towards the path junction by Exe Head there is no obvious path for just under a mile; in times of low cloud and poor visibility map and compass are a useful back-up.

At long last, the final stage! And what a finish: a long and – depending on the weather – potentially tough walk. From Simonsbath a rough and boggy way climbs towards the source of the River Exe, then crosses the edge of The Chains, Exmoor's highest and remotest ground. More high land is tackled over the Cheriton Ridge before easier paths follow the Hoar Oak Water. The final stretch enjoys wonderful views over the spectacular steep-sided wooded valley of the East Lyn River, with tantalising glimpses of the sea ahead. The lengthy descent into Lynmouth leads to a short walk past the harbour to The Esplanade and journey's end by the Pavilion, the Exmoor National Park Visitor Centre.

Walk towards the car park, passing the toilets and picnic area (benches but no tables). At the entrance to the higher parking area bear left on a narrow path (to Prayway Head) that runs along the top of Ashcombe Plantation (bluebells in May). The path descends to cross a stream under conifers and passes through a gate onto a field.

Exmoor is famous for its red deer herds, but you are more likely to see **roe deer** in these woods. This shy animal can be identified by its small size and white rump, highly visible when the animal is alarmed. The species was widespread in the Middle Ages and later disappeared before reintroduction to parts of England in the late 19th century.

Yellow-topped posts mark the line of the path above steep-sided **Ashcombe Bottom**. Pass through a gate and follow the bank-topped path across rough and broken ground, bearing left around the head of a small combe. Cross a dilapidated boardwalk, then a bridge, and then cross a stream; a few paces later turn right through the bank (very wet underfoot) then head uphill across damp and difficult ground, picking up occasional yellow-topped posts to find a wooden bridge over a particularly wet patch. Reach a hedgebank gate onto the open expanse of Great Ashcombe.

map continues on page 153

148

Turn left along the hedgebank to reach the Simonsbath–Lynton/Lynmouth road at **Prayway Head**. Turn right along the verge for 200yds, then cross over to find a layby, at the northern end of which turn left through a small gate. Immediately turn right to find another gate, then turn left alongside the hedgebank to reach a path junction. Although Exe Head is signed straight ahead the line of the path bears half-right (northwest) across **Dure Down**, aiming for the far corner, interspersed with clumps of woody rush (in places quite dense). ▶ Try not to stray too far to the right. Eventually a wire fence running along the Chains path appears away to the right; this path is met at **Exe Head** at a bridlepath junction, also marking the watershed.

The corner and the onward route thereafter is not visible until you are some distance across the field.

Despite the network of paths this is one of the remotest spots on Exmoor. **The Chains** – rising to 1599ft (487m) at the Chains Barrow, a little to the west of Exe Head – is a notoriously wet and boggy

Crossing the watershed: the upper Chains valley

Heading down the upper Hoaroak valley towards the Hoar Oak tree

moorland ridge that acts like a giant sponge, soaking up much of the high moor's annual rainfall of around 80in (2032mm). The rivers Exe, West Lyn and Barle all have their sources here. The Chains is home to Exmoor's most extensive area of blanket bog, sporting an impressive display of tufty white cotton grass in high summer.

Cross over and pass through the gate, signed to Hoar Oak. This long and rocky path drops steadily down the dramatic upper Chains valley; it is impossible to avoid getting wet feet where the infant Hoaroak Water emerges from Long Chains Combe. Eventually a line of beech trees in the valley bottom comes into view ahead, and the valley broadens.

High water variant

After heavy and prolonged rainfall it is difficult to cross the Hoaroak Water in the 'usual' place 250yds further down the valley (no bridge). In this event it is easier to cross the river here and pick up a narrow path that can be seen running along the east side of the valley, above the river, towards the Hoar Oak tree where it rejoins the usual route.

Just before reaching a gate across the path turn sharp right and drop steeply to wade across the river, then ascend towards the solitary **Hoar Oak** tree.

> The **Hoar Oak** (not, as one might expect, an ancient tree of enormous girth) marks the boundary of the Royal Forest, and is possibly one of an original line of oak trees on the boundary between the Forest and Lynton and Brendon Commons. The name comes from *har*, the Anglo-Saxon for 'boundary'. The present tree was planted to replace its predecessor – rumoured to have lived for 254 years – which was blown down in 1916. It stands on the Devon–Somerset boundary and you re-enter Devon at this point.

Turn left through a hedgebank gate (passing through the old Forest boundary: the wall was built on the orders of John Knight to mark the perimeter of his estate) and follow the grassy path ahead, parallel to a line of beautiful beech trees alongside the river. Meet a broader track (leading to Hoar Oak Cottage, which can be seen on the west side of the **Hoaroak Water**).

> The present **Hoar Oak Cottage** was built in the early 19th century, but there is earlier evidence of a medieval farmstead. It is likely that a simple summer shepherd's hut existed here – sheep being brought up to the moor to graze during the milder months – before more substantial and permanent buildings were constructed (as seen on the Ordnance Survey map of 1805). Now abandoned, it was owned and farmed by the Vellacott family from the late 18th century.

The path negotiates dense bracken near Hoar Oak Cottage

In times of poor visibility keep to the top of the ridge; do not drop eastwards into the valley of the Farley Water.

Bear right up the track, keeping left at a fork and heading north along the lovely **Cheriton Ridge** for around 2 miles (3.2km), with fabulous views west to Furzehill Common and east towards Brendon Common and, beyond that, what is known as 'Doone Country' – around the valley of Badgworthy Water – the area said to have inspired RD Blackmore's famous novel *Lorna Doone*; the author's grandfather was rector of St Mary's Church, Oare, from 1809 to 1842. ◄ At a hedgebank in the furthest right-hand corner of the ridge turn right down a stony track to meet the lane in the hamlet of **Cheriton**.

Turn left, signed to Hillsford Bridge. Pass Scoresdown Farm, beyond which the lane reduces to a very battered and rough track that descends extraordinarily steeply to pass pretty Old Scoresdown Cottage. Cross Smallcombe Bridge over the Hoaroak Water and turn right into the National Trust's **Combe Park**, part of the Watersmeet Site of Special Scientific Interest (SSSI), which includes one of the largest areas of semi-natural woodland in the southwest of England. The riverside path reaches the garden of the **Combe Park Hotel** then ascends to a junction; turn right to pass above the hotel, and along the top of a grassy slope. Descend through oak woodland to a footpath/bridleway junction; follow the footpath to meet the drive and car park.

Turn left to reach the Cheriton lane, and left again to meet the B3223 Simonsbath road at **Hillsford Bridge**, where the Farley Water joins the Hoaroak Water. ▶ Turn left again to cross the A39, with care, and proceed steeply uphill.

For Watersmeet cross Hillsford Bridge and turn immediately left to follow the Hoaroak Water to its confluence with the East Lyn river (under a mile).

Watersmeet House sits at the confluence of the Hoaroak and East Lyn, and was built as a fishing lodge by the Rev Halliday in 1832. In the late 18th century landscapes formerly considered wild and forbidding – moorland and mountain areas such as Exmoor and the Lake District – became fashionable when promoted by Romantic Movement authors and poets, such as Samuel Taylor Coleridge and William and Dorothy Wordsworth. Now under the care of the National Trust, the building has housed a tearoom for over a century. Two Moors Way walkers diverting for refreshment are best advised to retrace their steps to Hillsford Bridge to rejoin the route: there are paths from Watersmeet up the thickly wooded west side of the valley, but they are remarkably steep and taxing.

At the first sharp bend in the road keep straight ahead on a bridlepath to enter the National Trust's Watersmeet property. A long and steady ascent gains the earthworks at Myrtleberry South Iron Age enclosure (myrtleberry is yet another name for whortleberry). The path flits in and out of light oak woodland – in places with a very steep drop into the valley – with

map continues on page 157

Looking up the East Lyn valley from above Myrtleberry Cleave

extraordinary views over the dramatically incised and densely wooded spurs of the ravine. The East Lyn river has cut deeply into the moorland plateau, and here runs through Myrtleberry Cleave 800ft (250m) below the route of the Two Moors Way; it is spectacular, and a fitting finale. Soon a glimpse of blue sea appears in the deep cleft of the dramatic coastal hills at Lynmouth. A small descent into a tributary combe is rewarded with a very stiff zigzag ascent. Thankfully the occasional bench can be used to aid recovery, and the views are worth stopping for! Turn right as signed to negotiate Oxen Tor, and keep right at the next junction, heading downhill.

The long, steady descent to **Lynmouth** ends at a narrow and at times slippery tarmac path between pretty cottages to emerge onto the pavement of Watersmeet Road opposite the church of St John the Baptist by an engraved slab recording the opening of the Two Moors Way in May 1976. ◄

The names of the 34 people who lost their lives in the flood of 1952 are recorded in the church.

So is this the finish? Certainly not; a cross-county walk that starts at the sea should ideally end at the sea! So

Lynmouth comes into view, still a long way below the path

turn left to cross the A39 and walk down Riverside Road, marvelling at the view across the bay to the magnificent bulk of The Foreland. Pass the harbour to reach The Esplanade and the Rhenish Tower (beacon), destroyed in the floods of 1932 and rebuilt in 1954. If the National Park Visitor Centre in The Pavilion on The Esplanade is open make sure to sign their Two Moors Way/Devon Coast to Coast book to record your achievement.

The fishing village of **Lynmouth** became popular as a tourist resort in the 19th century, as evidenced by the number of elegant Victorian villas perched on the cliff-like hills rising from the coast. At the time the majority of visitors arrived by sea, inland communications being almost non-existent because of the inhospitable terrain; the Lynmouth Pavilion National Park Centre on The Esplanade is housed in the old steamboat terminal. It was not until 1828 that a road was built from Lynmouth up to the cliff-top settlement of Lynton, enabling visitors to

Looking towards the Rhenish Tower and harbour wall at Lynmouth

travel up the cliff by horse-drawn carriage. In 1890 the famous water-powered cliff railway between Lynmouth and Lynton opened – at a gradient of 1 in 1¾ – and it is still one of the town's biggest tourist attractions. But Lynmouth's biggest 'claim to fame' dates from August 1952 when a 40ft (12m) wall of water surged down the East Lyn valley – in the previous 24 hours nine inches (228mm) of rain had fallen on The Chains – destroying everything in its path.

Hopefully you will have built in time for a celebratory drink at the 14th-century thatched Rising Sun on the Harbourside before wending your way home.

Notes on how to plan your return from Lynmouth are given in the Introduction.

APPENDIX A

Route summary table

Stage	Start	Finish	Distance	Time	Maps	Page
1	Wembury Beach (SX 517 485)	Yealmpton, crossroads on the A379 in village centre (SX 579 518)	7½ miles (12km)	4hrs	Explorer OL20 South Devon; Landranger 201 Plymouth & Launceston, 202 Torbay & South Dartmoor	41
2	Yealmpton, crossroads on the A379 in village centre (SX 579 518)	Ivybridge, The Watermark, Erme Court (SX 637 562)	9 miles (14.5km)	4½hrs	Explorer OL20 South Devon; Landranger 202 Torbay & South Dartmoor	50
3	Ivybridge, The Watermark, Erme Court (SX 637 562)	Holne (SX 706 695)	13½ miles (21.75km)	7hrs	Explorer OL28 Dartmoor; Landranger 202 Torbay & South Dartmoor; Harvey Map Two Moors Way	59
4	Holne, crossroads in village centre (SX 706 695)	Dunstone Down, crossroads on southern end of Hamel Down (SX 704 759); or Widecombe-in-the-Moor, village green (SX 718 768)	7¼ miles (11.75km); or 9 miles (14.5km)	4hrs; or 4½hrs	Explorer OL28 Dartmoor; Landranger 202 Torbay & South Dartmoor, 191 Okehampton & North Dartmoor; Harvey Map Two Moors Way	71
5	Dunstone Down, crossroads on southern end of Hamel Down (SX 704 759); or Widecombe-in-the-Moor, village green (SX 718 768)	Chagford Bridge (SX 694 880)	9½ miles (15.25km); or 11 miles (17.7km)	5½ hrs; or 6hrs	Explorer OL28 Dartmoor; Landranger 191 Okehampton & North Dartmoor; Harvey Map Two Moors Way	80

Stage	Start	Finish	Distance	Time	Maps	Page
6	Chagford Bridge (SX 694 880)	The A377 south of Morchard Road (SS 756 043)	18 miles (29km)	8hrs	Explorer OL28 Dartmoor, 113 Okehampton; Landranger 191 Okehampton & North Dartmoor; Harvey Map Two Moors Way	101
7	The A377 south of Morchard Road (SS 756 043)	Witheridge, The Square (SS 803 145)	11 miles (17.75km)	5½hrs	Explorer 113 Okehampton, 127 South Molton & Chulmleigh (tiny stretch), 114 Exeter & the Exe Valley; Landranger 191 Okehampton & North Dartmoor, 181 Minehead & Brendon Hills; Harvey Map Two Moors Way	113
8	Witheridge, The Square (SS 803 145)	Knowstone, church steps (SS 828 231)	8¼ miles (13.25km)	4hrs	Explorer 114 Exeter & the Exe Valley; Landranger 181 Minehead & Brendon Hills; Harvey Map Two Moors Way	123
9	Knowstone, church steps (SS 828 231)	Tarr Steps (SS 868 361); or Withypool, General Stores (SS 846 335)	10 miles (16km); or 12¼ miles (19.7km)	4½hrs; or 5¾hrs	Explorer 114 Exeter & the Exe Valley, OL9 Exmoor; Landranger 181 Minehead & Brendon Hills; Harvey Map Two Moors Way	129
10	Tarr Steps (SS 868 321); or Withypool, General Stores (SS 846 335)	Simonsbath, Ashcombe car park (SS 774 394)	11 miles (17.75km); or 6½ miles (10.5km)	6hrs; or 3hrs	Explorer OL9 Exmoor; Landranger 181 Minehead & Brendon Hills, 180 Barnstaple & Ilfracombe; Harvey Map Two Moors Way	139
11	Simonsbath, Ashcombe car park (SS 774 394)	Lynmouth, The Pavilion on the Esplanade (SS 723 497)	11¼ miles (18km)	6hrs	Explorer OL9 Exmoor; Landranger 180 Barnstaple & Ilfracombe; Harvey Map Two Moors Way	147

APPENDIX B
Facilities along the Way

Place	Distance on	Hotel/b&b	Hostel/bunkhouse	Campsite	Pub/café	Shop	Cashpoint
Wembury		✓		✓ (off route)	✓ (off route)	✓ (off route)	✓ (at PO)
Brixton	5 miles (8km)	✓		✓	✓	✓	
Yealmpton	2½ miles (4km)	✓			✓	✓	✓ (at PO)
Sequer's Bridge	4¾ miles (7.5km)	No facilities					
Ivybridge	4¼ miles (6.75km)	✓		✓	✓	✓	✓
Red Lake Railway	8¼ miles (13.25km)	No facilities					
Scorriton	4½ miles (7.25km)	✓ (off route)			✓ (off route)		
Holne	¾ mile (1.25km)			✓ (off route)	✓	✓	
New Bridge	¾ mile (1.25km)	No facilities					
Bel Tor Corner	3 miles (4.75km)				✓ (off route)		
Forder Bridge	2 miles (3.25km)	✓ (off route)					
Dunstone Down	1½ miles (2.5km)		✓ (off route)				

Place	Distance on	Hotel/b&b	Hostel/ bunkhouse	Campsite	Pub/café	Shop	Cashpoint
Widecombe (1 mile off route)		✓		✓ (nearby)	✓	✓	
Grimspound	2¾ miles (4.5km)	No facilities					
Bennett's Cross	1½ miles (2.5km)		✓ (off route)	✓ (off route)	✓ (off route)		
Yardworthy	2¾ miles (4.5km)	No facilities					
Teigncombe	1¼ miles (2km)	No facilities					
Chagford Bridge	1¼ miles (2.5km)	No facilities					
Chagford	1 mile off route	✓			✓	✓	✓
Drewsteignton	5¾ miles (9.25km)	✓	✓		✓	✓	✓ (at PO)
A30	1¼ miles (2.75km)			✓ (off route)			
Hittisleigh	1¾ miles (2.75km)	✓					
Colebrooke link	4¼ miles (6.75km)	No facilities					
Clannaborough/A3072	3½ miles (5.5km)			✓ (off route)	✓ (off route)		
Morchard Road	1½ miles (2.5km)	✓ (off route)			✓	✓	
Morchard Bishop	3 miles (4.75km)	✓			✓	✓	

161

Place	Distance on	Hotel/b&b	Hostel/bunkhouse	Campsite	Pub/café	Shop	Cashpoint
Black Dog	3¾ miles (6km)	✓			✓ (off route)		
Washford Pyne	1¾ miles (2.75km)	No facilities					
Witheridge	2½ miles (4km)	✓		✓ (off route)	✓	✓	✓ (at PO)
Backstone Cross	5¾ miles (9.75km)	No facilities					
Knowstone	2½ miles (4km)	✓			✓		
West Anstey	4½ miles (7.25km)	✓					
Hawkridge	3½ miles (5.5km)	No facilities					
Tarr Steps	2 miles (3.25km)	✓			✓		
Withypool	4½ miles (7.25km)	✓			✓	✓	✓ (at PO)
Simonsbath	6½ miles (10.5km)	✓			✓		
Prayway Head	1¾ miles (2.75km)	No facilities					
Cheriton	5 miles (8km)	No facilities					
Hillsford Bridge	1½ miles (2.5km)			✓ (off route)	✓ (off route)		
Lynmouth/Lynton	3 miles (4.75km)	✓		✓ (off route)	✓	✓	✓

Mountain ash in autumn, Dartmoor

APPENDIX C
Selected accommodation

Wembury
B&Bs
See websites and Appendix D

Brixton
B&Bs
See websites and Appendix D

Yealmpton
B&Bs
See websites and Appendix D

Ivybridge
The Sportsmans Inn
www.thesportsmansinn.co.uk
Tel 01752 892280

Scorriton
The Tradesman's Arms
www.thetradesmansarms.co.uk
Tel 01364 631206

Holne
Church House Inn
www.dartmoorchurchhouseinn.co.uk
Tel 01364 631208

Widecombe-in-the-Moor (off route)
B&Bs
See websites and Appendix D

Chagford (off route)
The Three Crowns Hotel
www.threecrowns-chagford.co.uk
Tel 01647 433444

Chagford (off route)
The Globe Inn
www.theglobeinnchagford.co.uk
Tel 01647 433485

Sandy Park
The Sandy Park Inn
www.sandyparkinn.co.uk
Tel 01647 433267

Drewsteignton
The Drewe Arms
www.thedrewearmsinn.co.uk
Tel 01647 281409

Morchard Road
The Devonshire Dumpling
www.devonshire-dumpling.com
Tel 01363 85102

Black Dog
The Black Dog Inn
www.theblackdoginn.co.uk
Tel 01884 860336

Witheridge
The Mitre Inn
www.the-mitre-inn.co.uk
Tel 01884 861263

Knowstone
B&Bs
See websites and Appendix D

Tarr Steps
Tarr Farm Inn
www.tarrfarm.co.uk
Tel 01643 851507

Withypool
The Royal Oak Inn
www.royaloakwithypool.co.uk
Tel 01643 831506

In the summer months many paths in the Mid Devon section will become overgrown but still easy to walk (Stage 7)

Simonsbath
Exmoor Forest Inn
www.exmoorforestinn.co.uk
Tel 01643 831341

Simonsbath
Simonsbath House Hotel
www.simonsbathhouse.co.uk
Tel 01643 831259

Lynmouth/Lynton
B&Bs
See websites and Appendix D

Useful websites

www.dartmooraccommodation.co.uk
www.exmoor-accommodation.co.uk

www.ramblefest.com
This website is not bang up to date, but at the time of writing is the best source of information available. Please contact Ramblefest with any information about new services or accommodation along the route.

www.independenthostelguide.co.uk
Options close to the end of Stages 2 and 4.

www.yha.org.uk
Limited options along the way, most of which involve a significant detour off the route.

See also village and general websites listed in Appendix D.

APPENDIX D
Useful contacts

Supplies and refreshments

Wembury
The Old Mill Café
Tel 01752 863280

Brixton
www.brixton-village.co.uk

Yealmpton
Market Street Café
Tel 01752 880560

Ivybridge
The Watermark
www.ivybridgewatermark.co.uk/
information-centre
Tel 01752 892220

Holne
Holne Community Shop and Tearoom
Tel 01364 631188

Widecombe
www.widecombe-in-the-moor.com

Chagford
www.visitchagford.com

Drewsteignton
www.drewsteigntonparish.co.uk
Post Office Stores
Tel 01647 281220

Morchard Bishop
www.morchardnet.org.uk
Church Street Stores & Café
Tel 01363 877826

Witheridge
Witheridge Newsagents
Tel 01884 860815

Knowstone
The Masons Arms
www.masonsarmsdevon.co.uk
Tel 01398 341231

Withypool
www.withypoolexmoor.co.uk
Post Office and General Stores
Tel 01643 831178

Holiday companies
Celtic Trails Walking Holidays
www.celtic-trails.com
Tel 01291 689774

Contours Walking Holidays
www.contours.co.uk
Tel 01629 821900

Encounter Holidays
www.encounterwalkingholidays.com
Tel 01208 871066

Let's Go Walking
www.twomoorswaywalkingholidays.com
Tel 01837 880075

Macs Adventure Walking Holidays
www.macsadventure.com
Tel 0141 530 4018

Westcountry Walking Holidays
www.westcountry-walking-holidays.com
Tel 0330 350 1348

Luggage transfers
Luggage Transfers
www.luggagetransfers.co.uk
Tel 0800 043 7927/01326 567247

Moorland rescue services
Dial 112 or 999 and ask for the police

www.dartmoor-rescue.org
www.exmoor-srt.org.uk

Tourist information
Dartmoor National Park Authority
Visitor Centre
Tavistock Road, Princetown
Yelverton PL20 6QF
Tel 01822 890414
www.dartmoor-npa.gov.uk
www.visitdartmoor.co.uk

Devon County Council
www.exploredevon.info

Exmoor National Park Authority
Visitor Centre
The Pavilion, The Esplanade
Lynmouth EX35 6EQ
Tel 01598 752509
www.exmoor-nationalpark.gov.uk
www.visit-exmoor.co.uk

Ivybridge Tourist Information
The Watermark
Erme Court
Ivybridge PL21 0SZ
Tel 01752 892220
www.ivybridgewatermark.co.uk/
information-centre

Long Distance Walkers Association
www.ldwa.org.uk

Lynton & Lynmouth Tourist
Information Centre
Town Hall
Lee Road
Lynton EX35 6BT
Tel 01598 752225
www.lynton-lynmouth-tourism.co.uk

Plymouth Tourist Information Centre
Plymouth Mayflower
3–5 The Barbican
Plymouth PL1 2LR
Tel 01752 306330
www.plymouth.gov.uk/
touristinformationcentre

South Devon
www.visitsouthdevon.co.uk

Two Moors Way Association
www.twomoorsway.org

Travel information
www.firstgreatwestern.co.uk
www.journeydevon.info
www.nationalexpress.com

Traveline
www.travelinesw.com
info@travelinesw.com

Contact details for local bus companies, taxi firms and so on are given in the Introduction under 'Getting there – and getting away'.

APPENDIX E

Stamp stations

In 2006, to mark the 30th anniversary of the Two Moors Way (and its extension to Wembury to form the Devon Coast to Coast), two Radio Devon journalists (www.bbc.co.uk/radiodevon) set up a stamp trail along the whole route. The passport can still be downloaded (www.bbc.co.uk/devon/images/two_ways_passport.pdf) but the website list of stamping stations is not up-to-date; and the 'Certificate of Achievement' (originally obtainable from the Two Moors Way Association) is no longer available. At the time of writing the Old Mill Café at Wembury did not have a stamp (having changed hands in 2013). There is no longer a village shop at West Anstey. Please note too that some of the stamps held at the locations listed below are becoming quite frail!

The Exmoor National Park Visitor Centre in The Pavilion at Lynmouth does, however, have both a stamp and a Visitors' Book for south-to-north 'completers' to sign at the end of the walk. Those wishing to collect stamps along the way are advised to carry their own small notebook for that purpose.

Note that the recently revived Two Moors Way Association (www.twomoorsway.org) is planning to reintroduce the passport and stamps along the whole Devon coast-to-coast route.

Stamp station locations (April 2016)

Wembury
Old Mill Café, Wembury Beach (under development)

Yealmpton
Market Street Café, Yealmpton

Ivybridge
The Watermark, Erme Court

Holne
Community Shop and Tearoom

Drewsteignton
Post Office Stores, The Square

Morchard Bishop
The London Inn

Witheridge
Newsagents, 16a The Square

Knowstone
Masons Arms and in the porch of the parish church

Withypool
Post Office and General Stores

Simonsbath
Simonsbath House Hotel

Lynmouth
The Pavilion, The Esplanade

APPENDIX F
Further reading

Alton, Chris. 'Metropolis to Moor' *Dartmoor Magazine* 104 (Edgemoor Publishing, 2011)

Andrews, Robert. *The Rough Guide to Devon & Cornwall* (Rough Guides, 2004)

Baker, Nick. 'Nick Baker's Autumn Watch' *Dartmoor Magazine* 96 (Edgemoor Publishing, 2009)

Baker, Nick. 'Nick Baker's Dartmoor Autumn' *Dartmoor Magazine* 100 (Edgemoor Publishing, 2010)

Belsey, Valerie. 'Toll houses and milestones' South Devon AONB website (2011)

Britain's Wildlife, Plants and Flowers (Reader's Digest, 1992)

Chapman, Chris, Parker, David and Priestley, Philip. *Secrets of the Moor* (Exmoor Books, 1992)

Crossing, William. *Guide to Dartmoor* Reprint of 1912 Edition (Peninsula Press, 1990)

Darlington, Luke. 'Keble Martin's Chapel' *Dartmoor Magazine* 95 (Edgemoor Publishing, 2009)

Dell, Simon. 'Keble Martin and the Ordnance Survey Curiosity' *Dartmoor Magazine* 111 (Edgemoor Publishing, 2013)

The Friends of Hoar Oak Cottage website www.hoaroakcottage.org

Gibson, Anthony. *With Magic in My Eyes: West Country Literary Landscapes* (Fairfield Books, 2011)

Hemery, Eric. *Walking Dartmoor's Ancient Tracks* (Robert Hale, 1986)

Hemery, Eric. *Walking the Dartmoor Railroads* (Peninsula Press, 1991)

Hemery, Eric. *Walking the Dartmoor Waterways* (David & Charles, 1986)

Hoskins, WG. *Devon* (David & Charles, 1972)

In the News *Dartmoor Magazine* 92 (Edgemoor Publishing, 2008)

Macadam, John. *The Two Moors Way* (Aurum Press, 1997)

Mee, Arthur. *The King's England: Devon* (Hodder and Stoughton, 1965)

Mee, Arther. *The King's England: Somerset* (Hodder and Stoughton, 1941)

Mercer, Professor Ian. *Dartmoor* New Naturalist Library (Collins, 2009)

Pearce, Brian. *Dartmoor The Official National Park Guide* (Pevensey Press, 2000)

Pearce, Brian. *Exmoor The Official National Park Guide* (Pevensey Press, 2001)

Rego, Mike. 'Bovey Tracey Earthquake shakes Devon' *Dartmoor Magazine* 104 (Edgemoor Publishing, 2011)

Red Belted Galloway with Saddle Tor beyond

Ridgers, Colin and Heather. 'Of Rabbits and Men' *Dartmoor Magazine* 110 (Edgemoor Publishing, 2013)

Roberts, James. *The Two Moors Way* (Cicerone Press, 1994)

Sale, Richard. *Dartmoor: the official National Park Guide* (David & Charles, 2000)

Sampson, Mike. 'Dartmoor rain 2013' *Dartmoor Magazine* 114 (Blackingstone Publishing, 2014)

Thomas, Tina. 'Chagford Pool' *Dartmoor Magazine* 95 (Edgemoor Publishing, 2009)

Viccars, Sue. *Dartmoor* Short Walks (Jarrold Publishing, 2003)

Viccars, Sue. *Exmoor* Short Walks (Jarrold Publishing, 2003)

Viccars, Sue. *North and Mid Devon* Pathfinder Guides (Crimson Publishing, 2011)

Viccars, Sue. 'Silent Woods and Ridges' *Exmoor: the country magazine* 30 (Halsgrove Magazines, 2005)

Viccars, Sue. 'Tarr Steps and Withypool' *Exmoor: the country magazine* 50 (Hoar Oak Publishing Ltd, 2010)

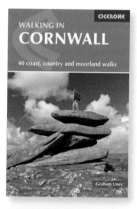
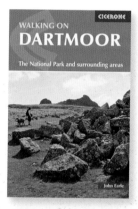
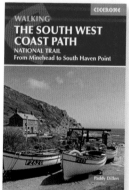
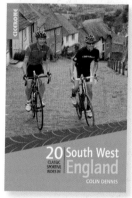

LISTING OF CICERONE GUIDES

SCOTLAND
Backpacker's Britain:
  Northern Scotland
Ben Nevis and Glen Coe
Cycling in the Hebrides
Great Mountain Days in Scotland
Mountain Biking in Southern and
  Central Scotland
Mountain Biking in West and
  North West Scotland
Not the West Highland Way
Scotland
Scotland's Best Small Mountains
Scotland's Far West
Scotland's Mountain Ridges
Scrambles in Lochaber
The Ayrshire and Arran
  Coastal Paths
The Border Country
The Cape Wrath Trail
The Great Glen Way
The Great Glen Way Map Booklet
The Hebridean Way
The Hebrides
The Isle of Mull
The Isle of Skye
The Skye Trail
The Southern Upland Way
The Speyside Way
The Speyside Way Map Booklet
The West Highland Way
Walking Highland Perthshire
Walking in Scotland's Far North
Walking in the Angus Glens
Walking in the Cairngorms
Walking in the Ochils, Campsie
  Fells and Lomond Hills
Walking in the Pentland Hills
Walking in the Southern Uplands
Walking in Torridon
Walking Loch Lomond and
  the Trossachs
Walking on Arran
Walking on Harris and Lewis
Walking on Jura, Islay
  and Colonsay
Walking on Rum and the
  Small Isles
Walking on the Orkney and
  Shetland Isles
Walking on Uist and Barra
Walking the Corbetts
  Vol 1 South of the Great Glen
Walking the Corbetts
  Vol 2 North of the Great Glen
Walking the Galloway Hills
Walking the Munros Vol 1 –
  Southern, Central and
  Western Highlands

Walking the Munros Vol 2 –
  Northern Highlands and
  the Cairngorms
West Highland Way Map Booklet
Winter Climbs Ben Nevis and
  Glen Coe
Winter Climbs in the Cairngorms

NORTHERN ENGLAND TRAILS
Hadrian's Wall Path
Hadrian's Wall Path Map Booklet
Pennine Way Map Booklet
The Coast to Coast Map Booklet
The Coast to Coast Walk
The Dales Way
The Pennine Way

LAKE DISTRICT
Cycling in the Lake District
Great Mountain Days in
  the Lake District
Helvellyn
Lake District Winter Climbs
Lake District: High Level and
  Fell Walks
Lake District: Low Level and
  Lake Walks
Lakeland Fellranger
Mountain Biking in the
  Lake District
Rocky Rambler's Wild Walks
Scrambles in the Lake District
  – North
Scrambles in the Lake District
  – South
Short Walks in Lakeland
  Book 1: South Lakeland
Short Walks in Lakeland
  Book 2: North Lakeland
Short Walks in Lakeland
  Book 3: West Lakeland
The Cumbria Coastal Way
The Cumbria Way
Tour of the Lake District
Trail and Fell Running in the
  Lake District

NORTH WEST ENGLAND AND
THE ISLE OF MAN
Cycling the Pennine Bridleway
Isle of Man Coastal Path
The Lancashire Cycleway
The Lune Valley and Howgills –
  A Walking Guide
The Ribble Way
Walking in Cumbria's Eden Valley
Walking in Lancashire
Walking in the Forest of Bowland
  and Pendle

Walking on the Isle of Man
Walking on the West
  Pennine Moors
Walks in Lancashire
  Witch Country
Walks in Ribble Country
Walks in Silverdale and Arnside
Walks in the Forest of Bowland

NORTH EAST ENGLAND,
YORKSHIRE DALES AND
PENNINES
Cycling in the Yorkshire Dales
Great Mountain Days in
  the Pennines
Historic Walks in North Yorkshire
Mountain Biking in the
  Yorkshire Dales
South Pennine Walks
St Oswald's Way and
  St Cuthbert's Way
The Cleveland Way and the
  Yorkshire Wolds Way
The Cleveland Way Map Booklet
The North York Moors
The Reivers Way
The Teesdale Way
Walking in County Durham
Walking in Northumberland
Walking in the North Pennines
Walking in the Yorkshire Dales:
  North and East
Walking in the Yorkshire Dales:
  South and West
Walks in Dales Country
Walks in the Yorkshire Dales

WALES AND WELSH BORDERS
Glyndwr's Way
Great Mountain Days
  in Snowdonia
Hillwalking in Shropshire
Hillwalking in Wales – Vol 1
Hillwalking in Wales – Vol 2
Mountain Walking in Snowdonia
Offa's Dyke Path
Offa's Dyke Path Map Booklet
Pembrokeshire Coast Path
  Map Booklet
Ridges of Snowdonia
Scrambles in Snowdonia
The Ascent of Snowdon
The Ceredigion and Snowdonia
  Coast Paths
The Pembrokeshire Coast Path
The Severn Way
The Snowdonia Way
The Wales Coast Path
The Wye Valley Walk

Walking in Carmarthenshire
Walking in Pembrokeshire
Walking in the Forest of Dean
Walking in the South
Wales Valleys
Walking in the Wye Valley
Walking on the Brecon Beacons
Walking on the Gower
Welsh Winter Climbs

DERBYSHIRE, PEAK DISTRICT AND MIDLANDS

Cycling in the Peak District
Dark Peak Walks
Scrambles in the Dark Peak
Walking in Derbyshire
White Peak Walks:
The Northern Dales
White Peak Walks:
The Southern Dales

SOUTHERN ENGLAND

20 Classic Sportive Rides in
South East England
20 Classic Sportive Rides in
South West England
Cycling in the Cotswolds
Mountain Biking on the
North Downs
Mountain Biking on the
South Downs
North Downs Way Map Booklet
South West Coast Path Map
Booklet – Minehead to St Ives
South West Coast Path Map
Booklet – Plymouth to Poole
South West Coast Path Map
Booklet – St Ives to Plymouth
Suffolk Coast and Heath Walks
The Cotswold Way
The Cotswold Way Map Booklet
The Great Stones Way
The Kennet and Avon Canal
The Lea Valley Walk
The North Downs Way
The Peddars Way and Norfolk
Coast Path
The Pilgrims' Way
The Ridgeway Map Booklet
The Ridgeway National Trail
The South Downs Way
The South Downs Way
Map Booklet
The South West Coast Path
The Thames Path
The Thames Path Map Booklet
The Two Moors Way
Walking in Cornwall
Walking in Essex
Walking in Kent
Walking in Norfolk

Walking in Sussex
Walking in the Chilterns
Walking in the Cotswolds
Walking in the Isles of Scilly
Walking in the New Forest
Walking in the North
Wessex Downs
Walking in the Thames Valley
Walking on Dartmoor
Walking on Guernsey
Walking on Jersey
Walking on the Isle of Wight
Walking the Jurassic Coast
Walks in the South Downs
National Park

BRITISH ISLES CHALLENGES, COLLECTIONS AND ACTIVITIES

The Book of the Bivvy
The Book of the Bothy
The C2C Cycle Route
The End to End Cycle Route
The End to End Trail
The Mountains of England and
Wales: Vol 1 Wales
The Mountains of England and
Wales: Vol 2 England
The National Trails
The UK's County Tops
Three Peaks, Ten Tors

ALPS – CROSS BORDER ROUTES

100 Hut Walks in the Alps
Across the Eastern Alps: E5
Alpine Ski Mountaineering
Vol 1 – Western Alps
Alpine Ski Mountaineering Vol 2
– Central and Eastern Alps
Chamonix to Zermatt
The Tour of the Bernina
Tour of Mont Blanc
Tour of Monte Rosa
Tour of the Matterhorn
Trail Running – Chamonix and
the Mont Blanc region
Trekking in the Alps
Trekking in the Silvretta and
Rätikon Alps
Trekking Munich to Venice
Walking in the Alps

PYRENEES AND FRANCE/SPAIN CROSS BORDER ROUTES

The GR10 Trail
The GR11 Trail – La Senda
The Mountains of Andorra
The Pyrenean Haute Route
The Pyrenees
The Way of St James – France
The Way of St James – Spain
Walks and Climbs in the Pyrenees

AUSTRIA

The Adlerweg
Trekking in Austria's Hohe Tauern
Trekking in the Stubai Alps
Trekking in the Zillertal Alps
Walking in Austria

SWITZERLAND

Cycle Touring in Switzerland
The Swiss Alpine Pass Route –
Via Alpina Route 1
The Swiss Alps
Tour of the Jungfrau Region
Walking in the Bernese Oberland
Walking in the Valais
Walks in the Engadine –
Switzerland

FRANCE AND BELGIUM

Chamonix Mountain Adventures
Cycle Touring in France
Cycling the Canal du Midi
Écrins National Park
Mont Blanc Walks
Mountain Adventures in
the Maurienne
The Cathar Way
The GR20 Corsica
The GR5 Trail
The GR5 Trail – Vosges and Jura
The Grand Traverse of the
Massif Central
The Loire Cycle Route
The Moselle Cycle Route
The River Rhone Cycle Route
The Robert Louis Stevenson Trail
Tour of the Oisans: The GR54
Tour of the Queyras
Tour of the Vanoise
Vanoise Ski Touring
Via Ferratas of the French Alps
Walking in Corsica
Walking in Provence – East
Walking in Provence – West
Walking in the Auvergne
Walking in the Cevennes
Walking in the Dordogne
Walking in the Haute Savoie:
South
Walks in the Cathar Region
Walking in the Ardennes

GERMANY

Hiking and Biking in the
Black Forest
The Danube Cycleway Vol 1
The Rhine Cycle Route
The Westweg
Walking in the Bavarian Alps

For full information on all our
guides, books and eBooks,
visit our website:
www.cicerone.co.uk

Walking – Trekking – Mountaineering – Climbing – Cycling

Over 40 years, Cicerone have built up an outstanding collection of over 300 guides, inspiring all sorts of amazing adventures.

Every guide comes from extensive exploration and research by our expert authors, all with a passion for their subjects. They are frequently praised, endorsed and used by clubs, instructors and outdoor organisations.

All our titles can now be bought as **e-books**, **ePubs** and **Kindle** files and we also have an online magazine – **Cicerone Extra** – with features to help cyclists, climbers, walkers and trekkers choose their next adventure, at home or abroad.

Our website shows any **new information** we've had in since a book was published. Please do let us know if you find anything has changed, so that we can publish the latest details. On our **website** you'll also find great ideas and lots of detailed information about what's inside every guide and you can buy **individual routes** from many of them online.

It's easy to keep in touch with what's going on at Cicerone by getting our monthly **free e-newsletter**, which is full of offers, competitions, up-to-date information and topical articles. You can subscribe on our home page and also follow us on **Facebook** and **Twitter** or dip into our **blog**.

Cicerone – the very best guides for exploring the world.

CICERONE

2 Police Square Milnthorpe Cumbria LA7 7PY
Tel: 015395 62069 info@cicerone.co.uk
www.cicerone.co.uk and **www.cicerone-extra.com**